The Book of
PRIMAL
SIGNS

"Symbols are like signposts directing us into the realm of the subconscious and the spiritual; they are flashpoints that stir emotions and trigger deeper—even divine—connections. But they also take on lives of their own, twining across times and cultures, and Nigel Pennick has always had his finger on their pulse. *The Book of Primal Signs* is a veritable thesaurus of traditional symbolism, spanning from prehistory to today. This is a vital guidebook to a hidden world that is, most thankfully and wondrously, still in plain view."

MICHAEL MOYNIHAN,
COAUTHOR OF *LORDS OF CHAOS*

The Book of
PRIMAL
SIGNS

The High Magic of Symbols

NIGEL PENNICK

Destiny Books
Rochester, Vermont • Toronto, Canada

Destiny Books
One Park Street
Rochester, Vermont 05767
www.DestinyBooks.com
Destiny Books is a division of Inner Traditions International

Text stock is SFI certified

Originally published in the United Kingdom in 2007 by Spiritual Arts and Crafts Publishing, Cambridge, Great Britain, under the title *Primal Signs: Traditional Glyphs and Symbols*

Library of Congress Cataloging-in-Publication Data
Pennick, Nigel.
  [Primal signs]
  The book of primal signs : the high magic of symbols / Nigel Pennick.
    pages cm
  Includes bibliographical references and index.
  Previously published as: Primal signs : traditional glyphs and symbols. 2007.
  ISBN 978-1-62055-315-2 (pbk.) — ISBN 978-1-62055-316-9 (e-book)
  1. Symbolism. 2. Symbolism in art. 3. Occultism in art. 4. Signs and symbols.
I. Title.
  BF1623.S9.P46 2014
  133.3—dc23
                                                    2013049857

Printed and bound in the United States by Lake Book Manufacturing, Inc. The text stock is SFI certified. The Sustainable Forestry Initiative® program promotes sustainable forest management.

10 9 8 7 6 5 4 3 2 1

Text design by Brian Boynton and layout by Debbie Glogover
This book was typeset in Garamond Premier Pro

All photographs are by the author except where otherwise noted. Other illustrations are by the author and from the collection of the Library of the European Tradition.

To send correspondence to the author of this book, mail a first-class letter to the author c/o Inner Traditions • Bear & Company, One Park Street, Rochester, VT 05767, and we will forward the communication.

CONTENTS

PRIMAL SIGNS, TRADITIONAL GLYPHS, AND SYMBOLS

If Providence allows me I shall tell you, reader, a little of the traditions of my ancestral land and of northern Europe, of the meaning of tradition, and of the things that make it what it is and that link it with the universal themes of human existence: of day and night; of tide and season; of birth, living, and death; of ideas and thoughts; of philosophy, knowledge, and faith. Things that are part of my being, as they were of my ancestors, who understood such matters as the basis for their lives in fishing, sailing, weaving, boot making, laying bricks, carrying, brewing, making music, nurturing their families, reporting the news, teaching, and fighting for their country. Here, embedded in this culture, are those human artifacts we variously call signs, markings, symbols, tokens, emblems, letters, characters, sigils, runes, badges, insignias, diagrams, tags, blazonry, hatchments, escutcheons, hieroglyphics, earmarks, ciphers, colophons, monograms, monomarks, talismans, labels, brands, and logos—what I will collect together under the rubric *glyph* in this book. But to use a single word that will stand for all these variant things is not to claim that they are the same. It is a higher-order taxonomy that saves laborious and repetitive explanation of the precise nature of the glyph each time any one is discussed. Often categorization is used by authors as a means to belittle the work of others, to attempt heroically or foolhardily to impose a unified theory on the matter under scrutiny, thereby superseding the achievements of all previous workers and rendering them invalid and obsolete. This is not my intention in this work, for to even attempt such a feat one must hold the naive belief that knowledge is finite and can be captured at a single stroke. For we are all stray singers in the world: things are ever changing, and perception is one of those things. Examples and instances are made here to illustrate the matter under discussion, not to make these particular examples and instances into iconic, definitive, literal representations. My work is wholly symbolic in intention and has never set out to impose a man-made order on the myriad aspects the world. The cosmos is pluralistic, and there is no one type of anything, for there are limitless interconnections between all things, and what we decide they are depends on our viewpoint. In just the arena of symbolic artifacts made by human hands, there is a rich panoply: cats' cradles, troll knots, and straw plaits; charms, reliquaries, bundles, spirit boxes, fetishes, sacred images, and diviners' boards; *omphaloi*, waystones, obelisks, perrons, and crosses; staves, wands, rune staffs, and scepters; talismans, badges of rank, medals, orders, crowns, and regalia; and religious, magical, and geomantic* paraphernalia: crafted things "in sign of a figure" as Sir Thomas Malory put it. A motto engraved on an Old English ring reads "In On Is Al" (in one is all), emphasizing that all things in existence are interconnected and part of the whole. This is the mystery of being in existence: separation and unity are one. Each individual instance of anything that comes into being is unique: no two things, however close they may appear, are identical, for they have a separate existence that marks them out as different, yet in one *is* all. This is the essence of all things: infinite plurality contributing to the whole. This book is a contribution toward an understanding of this mystery.

---

*Geomancy: the art of divination by Earth, and the meaningful placement of buildings and other human constructions upon the Earth.

A SYMBOLIC WORLD

A symbol is not a single thing that can be put in a box like a stone. In this present era of literalism, symbolism is given less value than it was in more spiritual ages. From the middle of the twentieth century, the presentation of pictures on a screen has become the main system of representation. This means that the literal image is the primary way to describe the world. That an image may signify more than what can be seen on the screen does not occur to the viewer. Each thing presented is a spectacle that goes no further than itself as an object, an artifact, or a logo advertising some product for sale. Essentially it is iconic. One cannot present the unseen on a screen. But beyond the literal stands the metaphorical: the viewed object is not there to represent itself, but some other, deeper meaning that cannot be communicated in words. In this case the symbol is a means of experiencing the eldritch world, the numinous, essentially a personal experience that is not transferable. At this point the seen symbol provides access to the unconscious, the collective, and the cosmic. Because of this access to the human unconscious, symbols are available for manipulation by unscrupulous clerics, politicians, businesses, and the military. By adopting and appropriating a symbol, these interest groups make the claim that they are the sole representatives of the spiritual quality of that symbol, such as when the United Kingdom's Conservative Party appropriated the flaming torch, symbol of liberty, as a logo.

Ancient religion in Europe appears to have been largely aniconic, and the gods viewed as symbolic. In the ancient Greek world, which included present-day Turkey, the goddess Hera was signified by a rough-hewn plank of wood. Aphrodite and Cybele were embodied in particular stones, and a serpent symbolized the god of healing, Asklepios (Aesculapius). Later, these deities were portrayed in human form. In central and northwestern Europe, the Celtic religion was without images before the influence of the Etruscans and then the Romans altered religious perceptions and practices. Aniconism is not restricted to the monotheistic and near-monotheistic religions, as some claim. Long before the Christian or Islamic religions came into being, the Celtic general Brennos is reported to have laughed when he entered the Greek temple at Delphi and saw the gods portrayed in human form.

The Jewish religion taught that the divine cannot be portrayed in an image. The new religions that worshipped the god of the Jews, first the Eastern Orthodox Church and, shortly afterward, the Islamic, followed Jewish practice and forbade images. Of course, all these religions had already smashed up the images and symbols belonging to other religions, often appropriating symbols where they could be absorbed into the new system of symbols and their explanatory myths. There was a fierce fight using violence over images in the Eastern Church, which went on for decades until it finally led to the reinstatement of image making and the development of the instantly recognizable Orthodox icon. This did not happen in the Mohammedan religion, and the prohibition was in many cases extended beyond religious images to pictures of anything. The reason for forbidding images of divine beings and powers is the knowledge that veneration of the divine power symbolized by an image can easily deteriorate into the worship of the image itself: the power it signifies can be thought to be present in the material. So when the image is not present and a symbol stands for the presence, then the possibility of this image worship is minimized. The early Jewish idea that their God created humans in his form leads to the conclusion that the divine power is in the form of a man. But if God is in human form and has the much written-about right hand, does God also have a heart pumping blood round his body and flesh supported on a skeleton, all composed of cellular tissues with a genetic origin in divine DNA? Clearly this is absurd, and taking this literally generates practices such as the worship of the Phallus Dei, leading people into a theological cul-de-sac.

Genuine spirituality challenges image making of all kinds, while not having an obsession with iconoclasm. It does condemn the worship of much more pernicious images, the basic structures of economic and political power. Spirituality sees through their outer images and observes the selfish motivations of those who profit from this power, while promoting eternal values that have nothing to do with mass-media hype. Unlike politics and commerce, true spirituality is not subject to the ever changing whims and fancies of the fashion and advertising industries, which, indeed, are driven by image. Fashion and advertising, the public faces of the military-industrial complex, are always on the lookout to find new things to co-opt and use to keep the profits rolling in. In the last few years, the fashion-advertising industry, extending its plundering of various ethnic identities, co-opted certain external elements of religious identities as a further way of branding mass-produced products. This image is sanitized, censored, and of course dumbed down, and with its spiritual implications completely obliterated, falsely appears to be spiritual while serving only to profit those who have appropriated the copyright.

The identity of any authentic and autonomous movement can be submerged in the corporate image, which, although created partly from the original, does not contain any of the objectives, purposes, or meanings of that original. By focusing on the external appearance and using it to promote the interests of the business that owns it, the corporate image actually works to destroy the thing that it portrays. All that is left of the original is the external appearance, like the famous icon Che Guevara reduced to an image on a T-shirt or a cola bottle, purchased and consumed by people who do not know who he was or what he stood for. His image is used for profit by the very capitalists whom he fought against his whole life and died trying to defeat. But although the image can be consumed and subverted by the fashion-advertising industry, the principles or beliefs subverted in this way may not be disposed of so easily. If any movement co-opted by the fashion-advertising industry continues once it has ceased to be fashionable—as if the fashionable

Fig. I.I. T-shirts on sale, Cambridge Market, 2005

fad had never existed—then it is authentic. But if it is destroyed once the fashion-advertising industry moves on to plunder the next culture, then it was no more than an empty image and deserves to fade away into oblivion. On sale in England's Cambridge Market in 2005, the T-shirts shown in figure I.1, in addition to an image of Che Guevara, bear images of the Soviet Communists' hammer and sickle, a parody of the Adidas logo as a cannabis leaf, dead music heroes, and personifications of death, rude ironic texts, a tiger's head, the coat of arms of the City of London; and the escutcheon of the University of Cambridge.

SIGNS OF THE TIMES

We live in an abnormal time when powered machines are preferred in every context, even when handwork, which uses no fuel and does not add to global climate change, is possible to achieve the desired result. The hand-pushed lawnmower is almost unknown now, and few use a hand-powered drill, auger, or brace-and-bit. Foot-powered lathes and sewing machines have ceased to be used, and even grindstones have electric motors. Wheelbarrows with petrol engines carry materials, road sweepers ride huge fuel-driven machines instead of sweeping with a broom, and fallen leaves are blown away in autumn—at the end of the growing year—by powered blowers instead of sweeping by hand. The ancient carving of the chained devil in Pottergate, York, is surrounded by electrical cables, an unintended irony that shows our state of bondage to them (fig. I.2).

Fig. I.2. Bound devil, corbel on building in Stonegate, York

Of course, this profligate use of fuel and materials would not be sustainable even if it only meant that the sources of fuel and materials were used up. But in addition to resources being needlessly depleted, the pollution caused by using them is fueling catastrophic global climate change, too. So it is doubly destructive to use power tools needlessly. As John Ruskin wrote as long ago as 1869 and quoted in 1906, "There being three great classes of mechanical powers at our disposal, namely, (a) vital or muscular power; (b) natural mechanical power of wind, water, and electricity; and (c) artificially produced mechanical power; it is the first principle of economy to use all available vital power first, then the inexpensive natural forces, and only at last to have recourse to artificial power" (Ruskin 1906, 169). Ruskin's wise observations went unheeded. Traditional economics, using locally available materials and the power of the human body, animals, wind, and water, grounded in a spiritual understanding of the human being's place in the scheme of things, is not destructive on the same global scale as the use of fuel-driven, money-based, industrially manufactured machines and materials.

Historically, each of the elements of what are now called traditional life, art, and craft came into existence through practice, by the assemblage of components, each of which has a more or less natural form. Traditional making and building is *organic* in the real sense, the true meaning of the word hijacked by twentieth-century architectural modernists to mean something quite the opposite. The basic elements of traditional building in Europe are a frame or walls of timber, a roof of bark, thatch, or wooden shingles, and wooden doors and window shutters. Local variations within the general principles of European building emerged out of local conditions. They signify the local in a symbolic sense, too, for they serve as a focus of local identity. They reflect the local because they are constructed of local materials, chosen in order to last as long as possible and provide the best environment in relation to the location. Thus the several English traditions of building, emergent from local conditions, are distinct and remain potent signifiers of Englishness, replete with symbolic meaning.

Place is a significant element of traditional culture, and time is a part of place. The orientation of buildings for liturgical and practical reasons is universal in traditional culture. In addition to the liturgical necessity of eastern altars in churches, secular buildings were located according to prevailing winds and more esoteric considerations now recognized as geomantic. Most medieval college libraries in England faced "east and west," for example, sixteen in Cambridge and Oxford (Willis and Clark 1886, vol. 3, 414–15; Pennick 2005b, 24–29). Since the 1840s the dislocation of time brought about by centralized time zones has paralleled a diminishing awareness of place and direction. Figure I.3, taken at Bromyard in Herefordshire in summertime, shows

Fig. I.3. Solar time shown by the gnomon's shadow, compared with clock time on a wristwatch set to British standard time. Bromyard, Herefordshire, 2001.

the dislocation between actual *local apparent time* (*sun time*), measured directly from the shadow cast by the gnomon on a sundial, and official clock time, based on a theoretical *mean time* at the Greenwich Meridian, far to the east, an inaccuracy compounded by an extra hour added on for "daylight saving."

In the historical development of European traditional architecture, the decorative or ornamental parts are integral with the structure, being derived either directly from the techniques of construction, as a skillful development of them, or as the results of rites and ceremonies that are also an essential element of the construction and use of buildings. Traditional ornament was denigrated during the twentieth century by futurist-inspired, machine-loving architectural theorists who claimed puritanically that only machine-made blank surfaces were morally proper and that the authoritarian brave new world of the future would be devoid of ornament and the decorative arts. Part of the underlying reason for this crusade against art was the mistaken belief that if one destroys all meaningful cultural references to local identity, then one will abolish human conflict by making all people the same.

But the Latin word *ornare,* from which *ornament* comes, means to make fit, to prepare a place for the entry of the divine, bedecking it with offerings that symbolically reflect the spiritual powers invoked.

Traditional ornament makes permanent the remains of otherwise transient adornment from times of festivity. Garlands, flowers, fruits, leaves, flags, birds, skulls, bones, and other sacred and secular emblems of ownership and authority adorn buildings in permanent form in metalwork and stone on temples, churches, and public buildings, while paint, carved wood, and pargeting serve the vernacular. These are formalized in such a way that they enhance the function of the buildings in physical, symbolic, and cultural ways. A garlanded ram's head carved in stone on an eighteenth-century classical building in Bath shows the form well (fig. I.4). On page 199 there is an illustration of a carved stone representation of a garland made of a skull, the bones of the human skeleton, and hourglasses, all symbols of passing time, on the Oostkerk in Middelburg, the Netherlands.

Fig. I.4. Stone-carved classical garlands and ram's head, Bath

Although it is a human trait to seek the simplest solution to understanding the world, some people like to seek other, less plausible explanations. Often, they accept what they have been told, without thought and without question, and teach it to others as if it were the truth. The medieval English philosopher William of Occam (1270–1347), known by the epithet of "Unique and Invincible Teacher," is best remembered for his Latin razor: *"Entia non sunt multiplicanda,"* literally, "Entities are not to be multiplied." This means that when we are seeking the cause of a problem, we must be as sharp as a razor, slashing through the temptation to complicate matters, and first look at the simplest, the most obvious answer to our question. If we fail to do this, then we will be led away from a proper sequential process of investigation and fail to grasp the essentials. Of course, we must ask that question and not believe uncritically what we have been told. The meaning of these signs depends wholly on the context in which they were made and the context in which they are used; as William Richard Lethaby noted, they are a "code of symbols, accompanied by traditions which explained them" (Lethaby 1891, 2). A symbol denotes being in the world, unlike a sign, which denotes *the* being or *the* world. The symbol includes the observer, whereas a sign does not. Symbols permit us to progress consciously from the externally perceived form of a given phenomenon toward its essence. Symbols do not exist to be interpreted or decoded: they draw the observer inward to participate in the world of spirit (fig. I.5).

National Pageant, Scottish National Exhibition, Edinburgh, Celtic Groups Section—Oscar (son of Ossian) with Fionn's Dogs and Standard Bearer

Fig. I.5. Postcard recording the National Pageant, Scottish National Exhibition, Edinburgh, 1908, with costumed performers led by women playing traditional musical instruments and with a Scots glyph on the banner. The Library of the European Tradition.

PART I

Traditional Glyphs, Signs, Sigils, and Symbols in Practice

It is better to work for ten days on one item than to produce ten items in one day.

JOSEF AUGUST LUX, 1905

As they are creations of human consciousness, the perceived differences between particular glyphs or signs are a combination of geometric recognition and semantics. The change in the names and meanings of signs through time and between cultures indicates that they do not have fixed, archetypal meanings that come from the deepest unconscious or otherworldly sources. It is the nature of glyphs that there is ever an interaction between similar forms that forges a link between their meanings, the result of human perception that is structured to extrapolate meaning from fragments of the perceived world. Few glyphs, symbols, and signs are subject to agreement, for cultural context defines meaning. Euclidean geometry is indeed a matter that transcends culture: for instance, there can be no argument that a circle's radius fits into the circumference six times (Pennick 1980c, 2005b). From this geometric property of the circle, *ad triangulum* geometry is derived, as are glyphs such as the *Magen David* (Star of David), so closely and so long associated with Judaism. But beyond the immutable geometric forms, the nuances of convention determine the current interpretation of any sign. A significant element in the modern mythos of signs is a search for ancient wisdom, generally linked to the search for national or spiritual identity. Various theories assert that all glyphs originated in the glyphs of primal writings that can be traced back to ancient lost lands like Atlantis and Thule or Vedic India. Ancient myth and mythologized history tell of writing originating with deities or individuals, such as Hermes, Thoth, Adam, Woden, Ulfilas, and Cyril. Deities such as Seshat, Thoth, and Woden have been venerated as guardians of their various sacred writings. Welsh bardic spiritual writings trace writing back to *y prif un awgrym ar bymtheg* (the sixteen primal symbols) (Ab Ithel 1867, I, 80–81) (fig. 1).

There are cultural ascriptions to the origins of alphabets used in liturgy and magic, such as the runes, Ulfilas's Gothic alphabet, and

Fig. 1. The Welsh sixteen primal signs.
The Library of the European Tradition.

Church Slavonic (Pennick 1995a, 5–11). Examples also include sigils based on late antique practice, especially Byzantine, making monograms out of names, which was used widely in both ecclesiastical circles, the Gothic (Arian) church and the Slavonic (Russian/Bulgarian, etc.) Orthodox church, and the monogram of London on Anglo-Saxon coins. Gothic art in the sense of high medieval Christian art developed monograms used as sigils for the epithet and name of Jesus and Mary (Pennick 1991b, 69; Pennick 1996b, 88–93). And in rune craft, runes are combined to make bind runes, whose runic meaning often transcends that of the individual runes that compose them.

Alphabets are derived from pictograms and glyphs that stand for actual things or actions as well as phonetic sounds (Pennick 1991b, 1–6; Drucker 1995, 22–48). The modern Western alphabets (including Hebrew, Greek, Roman, Cyrillic, and Arabic) owe their source to an ancient Canaanite script. This developed into two major versions, Phoenician and Aramaic. Alphabets to the east of Syria were derived from the Aramaic, while those to the west, from Phoenician (Drucker 1995, 44–47). Hence the ancient alphabets of Europe, including North Italic, Runic, Gothic, Church Slavonic, and the many medieval magical alphabets, including the Welsh bardic alphabet Coelbren, have Phoenician roots. The Ogham characters used in early Christian Ireland and later by the bards are not an alphabet with characters, but a positional cipher based on an alphabet (Pennick 2000a, 1–25, fig. 6). The Oghams are linked closely with tree lore, and only in this aspect do they relate to the alphabetic systems of northern Europe. The Aibítir of the Gaeilge and Gaelic languages is actually an alphabet, as is the Coelbren y Beirdd of Wales (fig. 2), which was derived ultimately from the Phoenician script (Pennick 1991b, 123–70; Pennick 2000a, 78–81). And there are other means of transmitting culture, such as the Western

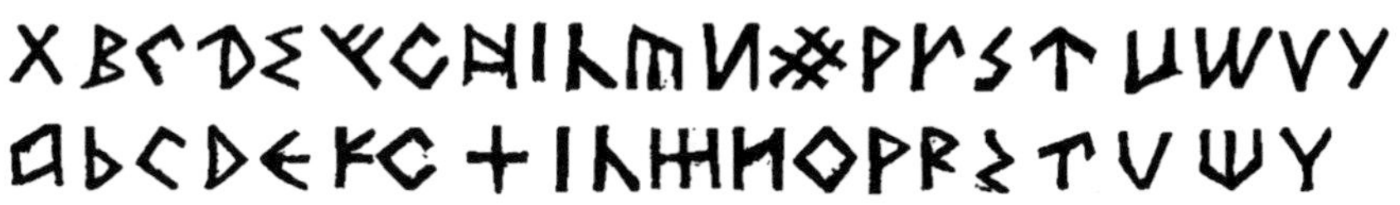

ᚷᛒᚲᛑᛖᚲᚲᚺᛁᛚᛗᚢᛨᛈᚱᛊᛏ ᚢᚹᚡᚤ
ᚨᛒᚲᛑᛖᚠᚲ ᛏᛁᚴᚻᚺᚺᛟᛈᚱᛉᛏᚢ ᚥᚤ

Fig. 2. Coelbren y Beirdd.
The Library of the European Tradition.

Fig. 3. Western musical notation: the traditional tune "Lillibulero."
The Library of the European Tradition.

notation of music, which works in an entirely different way from any alphabet or pictographic system (fig. 3).

THE RUNES

In the European tradition, the runes have a special place. The alphabetic glyphs we call runes are what appear in the mind when the word *rune* is heard. And in a book about primal glyphs, this aspect is, of course, of primary concern. However, the word is derived from older words in ancient European languages meaning "mystery" and "secret." A rune is not just a letter of an alphabet; it can be a song, an incantation, or an invocation as well as a glyph pregnant with symbolic meaning, either as an alphabet letter, an ideogram, or a symbol, in some cases all at the same time. Derived from ancient prealphabetic glyphs like the *hallristningär* of Scandinavia from as far back as 1300 BCE (Elliott 1959, 63–64) and combined with other glyphs from older alphabets, mainly the North Italic or Etruscan, the runes combine the phonetic meanings of alphabetic letters and pictographs and ideographic signs (fig. 4).

Originating as characters carved on wood and stone or inscribed in metalwork, the runes are angular forms. Their dimension in human consciousness is recalled by the story of Odin hanging himself on a tree for nine days and nights, at the end of which he received the runes (*Hávamál* 137–39). "Hidden runes shalt thou seek, and interpreted signs; many symbols of might and power by the great Singer

Fig. 4. A selection of *hallristningär*, ancient Scandinavian rock-carved glyphs

painted, by the High Powers fashioned, graved by the Utterer of the gods" (*Hávamál* 142). This account of a shamanic experience, terrible and life-changing, is recognizable to any who have been through such an ordeal, willingly or by accident. The psychic trauma dismembers the old persona, and if the individual survives, he or she is reconstructed in a subtly different manner. Shamanism gives access to eldritch areas of being that can rarely be reached in everyday states of consciousness. Thus the runes, grounded in the eldritch, mediate between the various realms of understanding, description, and the unspeakable inner workings of the mind and the cosmos. The myth of Ymir is a metaphor for the oneness of living beings with the fabric of the Earth, a symbolic way that we humans can relate to our existence here (Pennick 2006a, 83).

The earliest complete runic "alphabet" has twenty-four characters and is known as the Elder Futhark or the Common Germanic Futhark (a *futhark* being the first letters of the rune row). Perhaps as old as 200 BCE, the Elder Futhark appeared in Central Europe and spread northward as far as the Baltic Islands and the Netherlands (fig. 5).

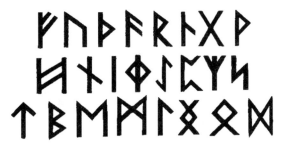

Fig. 5. The twenty-four runes of the Elder Futhark

From there the runes crossed to England, where the Old English rune row emerged, with twenty-nine glyphs. North of the River Humber, in the Anglian kingdom of Northumbria (now northern England and southern Scotland), the row expanded to thirty-three runes. In Denmark around the same time, the rune row was reduced to sixteen. This cut-down version of the futhark is now called the Younger Futhark. Later, a Swedish form of the runes was adopted, with the same letter order as the Greek and Roman alphabets. This continued in use until the eighteenth century.

The knowledge and use of the runes has been unbroken since their inception. In Sweden they were in everyday use as writing until the late seventeenth century, they were used in secret by wise women and cunning men, and they continued to count the days of the Julian calendar on wooden almanacs until that calendar was finally superseded, as late as 1921 in Estonia (fig. 6).

From the seventeenth century onward, scholars have studied the runes, as have antiquarians and archaeologists, who have collected and documented rare and choice artifacts bearing the glyphs, including medieval glyphs that are runes but are not accepted as such by those who have a narrow view of things. These I call nonfuthark runes, for want of a better description. They include craftsmen's marks, house

Fig. 6. Swedish runes, with their Roman letter equivalents.
The Library of the European Tradition.

marks, merchants' marks, and swan marks. A few of these German and Dutch glyphs have particular phonetic as well as symbolic meanings (Pennick 1999b, 77). During the nineteenth century, Guido List derived a new rune row from an earlier sixteen-rune row for his Armanen spiritual system, which subsequently entered the repertoire of Germanic occultism. These eighteen Armanen runes were based on the eighteen runic spells in *Hávamál*. The runes used today are predominantly from the Elder Futhark, as the system had been popularized in divination from the last third of the twentieth century. But the runes are not fixed, as history has shown, and there is always the possibility of the emergence of other runic glyphs as the next links in the unbroken chain. The structural glyph *mann* is a characteristic component in the timber-frame building technique called in German *Allamannisches Fachwerk*. Figure 7 shows a *mann* glyph on a building under construction at the end of the twentieth century at Soufflenheim in Alsace, France.

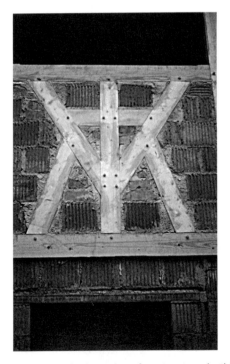

Fig. 7. *Mann*-glyph timber framing in a building
at Soufflenheim, Alsace, France

RUNIC LOGOS AND
DEFUNCT ORGANIZATIONS

Runes have been appropriated by various groups and organizations since the emergence of trademarks in the nineteenth century. German nationalists in particular espoused the runes in their emblems. The Nazi Schutzstaffel (Protection Corps, or SS) employed a double *sigel* (*sig*) rune as its sigil, and as a single glyph it appeared on the emblems of the Hitlerjugend, the Nazi version of the Boy Scouts. Scandinavian businesses, such as the Norwegian Design Centre and Finmar, have logos that allude to runic forms.

The most runic of glyphs used by a political movement in Great Britain so far was the double *K* of the Kindred of the Kibbo Kift or Kibbo Kift Kindred, which existed in Great Britain from 1920 until 1951.

Its sigil was a double *K* in runic style (fig. 8), a modern version of the *cen* rune, and the organization was known as the KKK. The use of the three letters *KKK* appears disturbing to some now because those letters are also the acronym of the Ku Klux Klan. The Kibbo Kift Kindred had no connection whatever with the Ku Klux Klan.

Fig. 8. The glyph of the
Kindred of the Kibbo Kift

The Kindred was an offshoot of the Boy Scout movement and was against nationalistic principles. In some ways a forerunner of later paganism, this KKK had four festivals in the year, based on the old English tradition. It celebrated the ancient spirit embodied in Merlin, Wayland Smith, Beowulf, and Hereward the Wake. The Kindred's main meeting annually was the Althing, held at Whitsuntide (the festival of the Pentecost), in the autumn was the Gleemote, and for midwinter, the Kin Feast. Each Easter a hike was made to Stonehenge. Preserved banners of the KKK have stylized emblems of Stonehenge and Old Sarum.

Later, the Kindred started to promote social credit politics, supported the Legion of the Unemployed, and conducted anticapitalist demonstrations. It disintegrated during World War II and was wound up officially in 1951. A rock opera, *The Kibbo Kift,* was performed at venues in Edinburgh and Sheffield in 1976.

But, as always, context is everything. The *K* was used first in this way in the nineteenth century by humorists such as Artemus Ward, who made ironic and playful deliberate misspellings of words in their comic writings. Perhaps the first use of the *K* in this way for an organization was by the first *krewe* of the New Orleans Mardi Gras carnival. The first krewe was the Krewe of Comus, set up in 1857; the Krewe of Rex followed in 1872, and subsequent carnival groups also called themselves krewes. Just before the city's destruction by hurricane in 2005, there were more than seventy krewes, bearing names from many cultural traditions, such as Bacchus, Choctaw, Cleopatra, Endymion, Jefferson, the L'il Rascals, Pontchartrain, Oshun, Zeus, and Zulu (Berry 2004, 301–2, 307). In 1865 the best-publicized *K* organization of all, the Ku Klux Klan, was formed in the manner of the maskers of the New Orleans carnival, but with the intention of maintaining white supremacy by force in the defeated territories of the Confederate States of America. The burning cross was the KKK sign, the call to arms employed by the Scottish highland clans. But the *K* name has never been restricted to the krewes or the Ku Klux Klan. In 1970s California the name Kwipment Krew described the roadies who worked for the Grateful Dead rock band. This deliberate misspelling to denote an in-group continues in the same way today, for example, the word *boyz,* used in a hip-hop context.

THE PITFALLS OF SYMBOLOGY

Among those who study signs and symbols, there is a tendency for observers to concentrate on a particular part of an ensemble, ignoring the rest. For example, when books on labyrinths show the labyrinth pattern of the pavement in San Vitale's church in Ravenna, Italy, they rarely show the seven other patterns that compose the octagonal mosaic. This is the principle of spectacle or the fetishism of the object, or "not to see the forest for the trees," as the popular adage puts it. Of course, to see anything is to make a selection. We can only see electromagnetic radiation over a small part of the continuum, and thus, for example, we do not see anything colored ultraviolet. Then our brains have been trained since birth to recognize certain shapes and forms in our environment, and it is difficult to see other kinds of things without a conscious effort. Then to describe what we see, we need language and a working taxonomy of the order of things as we perceive them. So there is much we miss and much we classify as distinct objects when they are integral parts of a larger whole.

In figure 9 the symbols on a traditional English wooden calendar—a clog almanac—are but a small fragment of the whole. The illustration is a small piece of an engraving that is the frontispiece to William Hone's *The Every-Day Book* of 1827. The Hone engraving is itself a copy of an illustration in Robert Plot's 1686 book, *History of Staffordshire.*

Plot himself chose a particular clog among the many that were in everyday use in the county where he wrote, and his artist engraved the clog as he saw it and in his style of woodcutting. Elsewhere in England and further abroad in Scotland, Scandinavia, and mainland Europe, peo-

Fig. 9. Clog-almanac glyphs. From *The Every-Day Book* by William Hone, vol. 2, 1827. The Library of the European Tradition.

ple were using clog almanacs of varying kinds in keeping up the day. Local and individual variations were limitless in a pluralistic, unregulated folk art. When I excerpted a small piece of the springtime section of Hone's illustration for this book on December 13, 2006, St. Lucy's Day, and put it here, I performed an act of further editing—a long trail of observation, selection, excerpting, and editing that went back at least 320 years. So any work on signs and symbols must inevitably follow the same principle. It is futile to claim that we can know and document everything that is and everything that is happening, that this or any other book is a complete and total documentation of the subject. To do so is to ignore the reality that the world is ever changing and its actuality can never be all collected together in one place, as the stately and magnificent Library of St. Victor once claimed to do. To act as if any of this were true is to fall into the trap of "the illusion of mastery" (Pennick 2006a, 11).

The same glyph can be used in many totally different contexts, depending on cultural meaning, and it is only explicable through the cultures and the history of the glyph within them, Lethaby's culture-laden "code of symbols" (Lethaby 1891, 2). Ephemeral uses, influential at the time but unobserved in the long run, can add new meanings to signs or obscure earlier ones. Some of the ephemera illustrated here show usages other than those of mainstream expectancy. Signs have been used as ornament, eye-catching patterns for advertising, and as logos for religious, political, and commercial purposes. But as the only permanent thing in the world is change, the meaning of things is also ephemeral. It is clear that there is a range of consciousness in their use, from deliberate symbolism to random prettiness. Ever since the invention of printing, glyphs have appeared on ephemera such as playbills, flyers, leaflets, posters, and greeting cards and longer-lived items such as trade union, political, and football supporters' banners; pop, rock, and hip-hop logos; and badges, coins, and medals. Few survive for any length of time, and those that do may sometimes bear images that need historical knowledge to understand. For example, the greeting cards in figure 10 were issued at about the same time. The stoic military Christmas card was sent home in 1916 by my great grandfather, Charles Robinson (1878–1947), who was serving in the British Army's 24th Division, which had fought

Fig. 10. Early twentieth-century greeting cards. Left: 1916 Christmas card from soldiers of the 24th Division of the British Army listing the engagements with the enemy that year: the Somme, Arras, Vimy Ridge, Loos, Neuve Chapelle, Ploogsteert, Kemmel, St. Eloi, Ypres, Hoog, and Hill 60. Sent by Charles Robinson, Pennick family archives. Right: a New Year card of around the same period, with good-luck charms: four-leaf clover, daisy, and swastika. The Library of the European Tradition.

that year on the Somme, at Arras, Vimy Ridge, Loos, Neuve Chapelle, Ploogsteert, Kemmel, St. Eloi, Ypres, Hoog, and over the notorious Hill 60. All are shown on the landscape behind the soldier, with a weary "where next?" as the header. The card with lucky charms, including a four-leaf clover, a daisy, and a swastika, was issued around the same time as a New Year greeting. Nobody without the relevant knowledge of history could correctly interpret them now.

Glyphs have been used in advertising as trademarks for a very long time. The Masonic Egyptian diamond of the London and North Western Railway Company, used until 1923, was designed by Joseph Locke for the Grand Junction Railway, its predecessor, in 1836 (Stretton 1909). Breweries were early users of easily recognizable glyphs: the red

Fig. 11. Old enameled metal advertising signs, including one with the red circle trademark of Echo Whisky.

triangle of Bass, the red circle of Echo Whisky, and the 1927 blue star of Newcastle breweries being prime instances (fig. 11).

In the 1890s the popular British magazine *Outing* used a dot in the middle of a circle as the *O* at the beginning of its name to double as a logo (fig. 12). This form of a roundel was taken up during the World War I in national colors to identify combat aircraft and remains in use today in modified versions.

Fig. 12. Logo of the magazine *Outing*, 1896, with roundel as the first letter. The Library of the European Tradition.

The Swastika Laundry in Ballsbridge, Dublin, used that sign as its logo between its setting up in 1912 and its closure in 1989. A battery-electric delivery van for the laundry is shown in figure 13 in an evening rush-hour traffic jam in Dublin in 1963.

The use of a circle with a horizontal bar, the roundel shown on a London underground train in figure 14, is now copyrighted worldwide by Transport for London. It originated in March 1905 as a wheel emblem designed by a "Mr. Crane" (the designer Walter Crane?) for the London General Omnibus Company (Lawrence 2000, 7–9; Reed

Fig. 13. Battery-electric delivery van of the Swastika Laundry,
Dublin, in traffic, August 1963.

Fig. 14. London underground train showing London Transport roundel.

2000, 14) and was extended to the underground and later all bus and tram (trolley) services in the city when London Transport was formed in 1933. "Roundel abuse," as it is called, the unauthorized use of this London transport glyph for other purposes, is now rigorously prosecuted by the copyright holders (David Leboff, personal communication).

There have been a number of suggestions for the antecedents of this famous London Transport roundel: the winged wheel of Hermes, a Hermetic glyph for water, an alchemical sigil of salt, the Earthy spirit in Anton Kirchweger's *Aurea Catena Homeri,* or Samuel Plimsoll's ship loading line, itself said to be derived from medieval Sardinian maritime practice (Koch 1930, 50, 65, 66; Masters 1955, 6; Lawrence 2000, 7, 35). Which, if any, is historically correct can never be known. Almost every other glyph we might encounter will also contain a comparable trail of history and plurality of meanings.

NEW NAMES,
NEW MEANINGS

It is historically documented through many cases that the names of signs and their ascribed significance and meanings alter through time, for copyrighting of signs and their registration as trademarks is recent in historical terms. The glyphs themselves may alter or be reidentified. For example, the arms of the kings of Frisia, first depicted in a Parisian armorial of 1528 as hearts, appear to have been water lily leaves in earlier Frisian heraldry (Commission of the Fryske Akademy 1956, 62). The corresponding relationship between leaves and spades in Central European and Franco-British playing cards is similar. The names used for the signs can change, too. For example, the names fylfot, *fyrfos, gammadion,* four-footed cross, tetraskelion, and cross potent rebated were used for centuries to label a sign now called the swastika. During the nineteenth century, Theosophical writers popularized Indian and Tibetan mystical ideas, and with them, the name *swastika,* meaning "all is well," arrived and superseded the earlier words. This glyph appeared in the works of Madame Helen P. Blavatsky and as part of the emblem of the Theosophical Society. Generally it was used as a lucky charm. In

Fig. 15. Vignette from *The Red Swastika* by Mark Harborough. The Library of the European Tradition.

Fig. 16. The swastika of the Krit Motor Car Company. The Library of the European Tradition.

1907 the Boy Scout movement adopted the fleur-de-lys and the swastika as its main signs (Taylor 2006, 125). A Boy Scout illustration from *The Red Swastika* by Mark Harborough is shown in figure 15.

Many of the logos adopted by American automobile manufacturers used traditional glyphs. The Krit Motor Car Company of Detroit used the swastika for some years in the early twentieth century (1909–1916) (fig. 16).

During World War I, the swastika was the logo for British National Savings Stamps (Pennick 1979b, 6; Taylor 2006, 126). After the official end of the war at the Armistice in 1918, the swastika was adopted by renegade elements of the German army that continued to fight in the Baltic countries. When they were defeated, some Baltic Freikorps soldiers who returned to then-anarchic Germany formed right-wing paramilitary units identified by the swastika painted on their helmets. From this it became the emblem of the German Workers' Party, which soon became the Nazi Party. At the same time, also in Germany, the left-wing artists of the Bauhaus adopted the sign in their early publications. Another artist, Adolf Hitler, used the glyph in a program of corporate design that was so successful that it superseded all previous meanings assigned to the swastika once the Nazi Party was elected to government. The subsequent violence and destruction that ensued from this meant that the sign then became almost wholly associated with war criminality.

In 1969 there was an attempt by a group of people in Cambridge, including myself, to reinstate the glyph to its traditional use, but still only a minority recognize these earlier meanings in Europe as well as its Asian connotations. Eight years later the punk band the Sex Pistols wore T-shirts printed in the colors and forms of the Nazi party flag as an outrageous provocation, especially in a video where Sid Vicious is shown walking through a predominantly Jewish quarter of Paris wearing the glyph. Clearly, however, they did not hold National Socialist views, using the sign for its shock publicity value, as they also did anarchist symbology. In twenty-first-century Britain, the pluralistic or multicultural nature of the country is also reflected in the variant usages of glyphs, signs, and symbols. The T-shirts from Cambridge Market shown in figure I.1 are instances of this. So in the same British city on the same day, an anti-Semitic fanatic may spray-paint a swastika on a Jewish tombstone, a latter-day Sid Vicious wannabe may wear a Sex Pistols swastika T-shirt, a Hindu may ritually paint a swastika on his house in a religious rite, devotees of a Tibetan Buddhist monastery may chant before a shrine bedecked with swastikas, and a Chinese woman may consult a printed calendar marked with swastikas. A Chinese calendar glyph from a publication printed in Birmingham in 2006 is shown in figure 17.

Fig. 17. Swastikas and yin and yang glyphs from a Chinese calendar, Birmingham, 2006. The Library of the European Tradition.

Fig. 18. Anti-Nazi graffito, Frankfurt-am-Main, Germany, 1992. Black swastika being shattered by a red boot.

And on a forgotten Saxon sundial moldering unnoticed on a church wall, a barely perceptible swastika may mark 7:30 a.m., the beginning of the working day. To each user the glyph has a different meaning, as it did to the anti-Nazi artist who spray-painted the graffito on a wall in Frankfurt-am-Main in Germany (fig. 18).

Names are a shorthand way of describing things, and every name originates somewhere and contains the concepts and ideology of the person who first used it. Names are familiar as identifiers for people, pets, and buildings, but it is seldom recognized that the names of abstract things also carry the same plurality identification that personal names do. Once a new name for a sign or image has become well established, then it also spawns an explanatory story based on the name rather than the original sign, and the new mythos about its meaning and origin may become the most widespread belief. The names used now for a number of glyphs and symbols originated in the first half of the twentieth century. In 1935 Walter Propping popularized the name *dag* for signs used on doorposts, doors, and window shutters, because they appeared to be a continuation of the Germanic rune *dag* (Propping 1935, 143–46). In 1936 a post bearing this sign taken from a house in Egton, Yorkshire, was donated to the Whitby Museum and called a witch post (Hayes and Rutter 1972, 87). Known before then as a speer post or heck post from its position as supporter of a screen next to the inglenook fireplace in the traditional Yorkshire farmhouses of Ryedale and Eskdale, it was called a witch post as the sign was deemed to protect against ill-wishing witchcraft. Now the name witch post is used without comment as though this has been its name since the days when the tra-

Fig. 19. Pargeted green man head, Clare, Suffolk

ditional farmhouses were built. In 1939 Lady Raglan wrote a paper in the journal *Folk-Lore* titled "The 'Green Man' in Church Architecture." Before her, these carven heads had not borne the name the green man, but had been called leafy faces or foliate heads by church photographer C. J. P. Cave (Raglan 1939, 47) (fig. 19). But Raglan's name was more evocative, even though she first used the name in quotation marks. Subsequently it has been absorbed into the language as the proper description, without the quotation marks, even though most are not colored. They have since become part of an entire mythic web that was not recognized earlier, for Raglan linked the heads with the sacrificed king from *The Golden Bough,* Robin Hood, Jack-in-the-Green, morris dancing, and the garland ceremonies at Castleton, Derbyshire.

THE PUBLIC USE OF GLYPHS

During World War II, the White Eagle Lodge, a spiritualist organization founded in 1936 by the medium Grace Cooke, paid for posters to be put up in the London underground and other places where people sheltered from the bombing. They depicted a cross of light— a sun wheel or Celtic cross—rising over the roofs of a darkened city. (This appears to be derived from an engraving in the Theosophical works of Jacob Boehme, published in Amsterdam in 1682, where the wheel of light is above an image of the New Jerusalem.) At the center of the White Eagle wheel was a six-petaled flower from which radiated twelve rays of light. Beneath this image was the slogan written in Art Deco capital letters: "The forces of darkness . . . halt! before the cross of light." Known as the Poster of Light, it was said to have originated in a spiritualist message sent by White Eagle, the spirit guide of the lodge. Designed by Cooke's daughter, Ylana Cooke, the poster gained the reputation as a talisman against enemy action, and stories circulated that houses where the poster was on the wall had avoided being bombed in the Blitz (Akhtar and Humphries 1999, 88–91). Yet only seventeen years after the obliteration of Nazi Germany, in 1962, the same glyph as on the Poster of Light appeared in Trafalgar Square at a public rally of an anti-Semitic political organization, the National Socialist movement, this time accompanying the Nazi-inspired slogan "Britain Awake" (fig. 20). It had been used before that by the White Defence League, founded in 1958 in London at the time of the Notting Hill race riots, seemingly having its origin in the 1928 French Fascist emblem the *croix de feu* (Davies and Lynch 2002, 270, 357).

In commerce the sun wheel had been used before 1930 in Great Britain as the record label of the British Zonophone Company. This sign is used in the early twenty-first century as a logo by a number of commercial companies.

Fig. 20. Rally of the National Socialist movement, Trafalgar Square, London, July 1962. Union flag and banner with sun-wheel glyph.

Around the same time as the National Socialist rally, the Campaign for Nuclear Disarmament (CND) commissioned Gerald Holtom to design a logo for its publicity. That logo was inspired apparently by the three-pointed star of Mercedes-Benz, designed by Gottlieb Daimler before 1900 (copyrighted 1911) (Wildbur 1966, 5). Derived from the semaphore positions for the letters *N* and *D* set within a circle, the CND glyph is in the form of the Northumbrian rune *calc* and the Younger Futhark rune *yr*. In the form of the three roots of Yggdrasil and hence the earth in which the roots grow, both runes are associated with the individual's death. *Yr* is the "death rune" of Teutonic magic (Pennick 1999b, 66, 71). It is not known whether Holtom knew its runic meanings. Following Rudolf Koch, who in 1930 called an earlier form of the sign "the crow's foot, or witch's foot," opponents of the CND called it the "pigeon's foot" or the "fork." Subsequently, the emblem became more widespread in its scope and was renamed by many the peace sign and was also known as the antimilitarist sign (fig. 21).

Fig. 21. CND glyph. Designer Gerald Holtom.

The anarchist *A* in a circle also dates from the same era. It is unusual in that the thinking behind the sign and its uses was published at the time it came into being. A writer in the Italian anarchist periodical *Rivista A* recorded the genesis of the *A* sign in Paris in 1964. The writer noted that the international bulletin *Jeunesses Libertaires* contained a proposal for a "graphic symbol" for

the whole of the anarchist movement, beyond the different tendencies and diverse groups and federations . . . there are two principal reasons: primarily to make wall graffiti and posters easier and more effective, and also to secure a wider presence for the anarchist movement in the eyes of the public and as a common denominator for all anarchist expressions and public appearances. . . . It was intended, as far as we were concerned, to find a practical medium that allowed on the one hand the reduction to a minimum of the time required to draw our slogans upon walls and on the other to choose a symbol sufficiently general to become accepted by all anarchists. (Anon. 1983, 12)

The writer in *Rivista A* noted that the "anti-militarist symbol" (the CND logo) was already widespread, and the capital *A* replaced it in anarchist circles. In 1966 Giuventu Libertaria, an anarchist group in Milan, Italy, adopted the sign, which then was reexported to Paris during the radical uprising of May 1968. From Paris it has spread worldwide, altering in later years so that the arms of the *A* sometimes break through the circle.

Many glyphs are continuously recycled over the years, being adopted by various interest groups as a convenient label under which to trade, campaign, compete, or fight. The selection of badges in figure 22 is a microcosm of the genres, each replete with meaning.

The anarchist *A* is in figure 22 at the top left, and beside it is the logo of the now-defunct British Social Democratic Party, its initials in blue and red on a white background, the national colors. Below these are

Fig. 22. Miscellaneous political badges, 1960–2000. Author's collection.

three CND badges from different periods, the oldest being the "badge of honor" issued to people who took part in a two-day march around Birmingham in October 1963. The "lunatic fringe" badge refers to the intemperate statements of Cambridge University archaeology professor Glyn Daniel in 1975 in the journal *Antiquity* against the Institute of Geomantic Research, calling institute members "the lunatic fringe of archaeology." The badge used imagery from the horror movie *The Giant Claw*. Women against Apartheid combined the Chinese yin and yang glyph with the European sigil of Venus, signifying the feminine. "Gays against Nazis" in black on pink, the color of the compulsory badges worn by gays in Nazi concentration camps, is combined with the arrow glyph of the Anti-Nazi League, itself derived from *Beat the Whites with the Red Wedge,* a famous Russian Communist poster of 1919 by El Lissitsky. The antinuclear group Pagans Against Nukes ("P.A.N") has an image of the head of the Great God Pan, who symbolizes the All threatened with destruction by nuclear power and nuclear war. Above this an old Labor Party lapel badge carries the symbols of physical and intellectual labor, the spade and the pen. In the middle is the flaming torch of liberty, overlain by the word "Liberty." The torch glyph was later appropriated in the days of Margaret Thatcher by Labor's opponents, the Conservative Party. Next to this is another CND glyph over a rainbow, but by now it has become the peace sign and bears a John Lennon song quotation. Below this is a direct message from *The Socialist Worker* newspaper: "Stop the war." The White Panthers, a short-lived white British revolutionary group based on the American Black Panthers paramilitary group, had an emblem of the beast on a purple background. "Resistance Shall Grow" refers to the secret underground bunkers built so civil servants and politicians could (in theory) rule the remains of Britain after a nuclear attack by the Soviets—the Regional Seats of Government (RSGs). Finally a black badge with "and white" may refer to a brand of whisky or be intended to indicate that the white working class has no political voice. The meaning is what the wearer intends. How much meaning a few badges can carry, and how rapidly can knowledge of these ephemeral meanings fade away and be forgotten.

Assemblage of spiritual artifacts including runic bracteate, bronze labyrinth, equal-armed cross with four-seasons glyphs, embroidered runic headband, moon ring, lunar crescent bracelet, beaded pentagram, *ziu*-rune sliver, Bury St. Edmund's pilgrim badge, ancient beads from King's Lynn, and thunderbolt and pattikeys (seeds) of an ash tree.

PART II

A Box of Glyphs

1. THE SUN, THE CIRCLE, AND THE SUN WHEEL

During the day, all is lit by the Sun, and light is the unity which rules everything and from which the darkness retreats.

JOHANNES LUDOVICUS MATHIEU LAUWERIKS

Fig. 1.1. Sun wheel

The roundnesses of the sun and the full moon give the circle a cosmic dimension. The disc of the sun is, of course, an archaic glyph, directly observed. It appears in ancient Egyptian art as an image on the heads of many divinities and was transferred thence in Christian art into the halo of divine and venerated beings. The circle can symbolize eternity—continuous, never beginning, and without end—and, like all nonverbal forms, it is ever open to rediscovery. In geometry, from the circle and using only a straightedge and compasses, all the major geometric figures can be drawn without measurement. Being derived from the circle, the *vesica piscis,* the equilateral triangle, the square, the hexagon, the pentagon, and other polygons all have direct and fixed relationships with one another, so the circle can be viewed as the primal figure of all geometry. In *The Seventh Key,* the alchemist Basil Valentine states:

> My son, take the simple and round body and do not take the triangle or quadrangle, but take the round body, for the round body is more related to simplicity than the triangle. Also it should be noted that the simple body has no angles, since it is the first and the last among the planets just as the sun is among the stars. (Valentine 1610, vol. 2, 207–8)

In the fifteenth century, the master architect Leon Battista Alberti wrote that the circle was an Egyptian symbol for time, another link with the sun by which time is measured (Alberti 1755, 169). In English folk tradition, it appears as a solar emblem. In her study of horse brasses in the early part of the last century, Lina Eckenstein traced their designs back to ancient times (Brears 1981, 43). In Kent she found that circular horse brasses were called sun brasses. The pargetted wall shown in figure 1.2 is from the Old Sun Inn in Saffron Walden, Essex. The identity of the figures is pluralistic: some label them Tom Hickathrift (Hiccafrith) and the Giant, and an older appellation is Gog and Magog (Maddren 1992, 36–37, 46; Hooper 2002, 62–63). Between the figures, the disc represents the sun, the name of the former inn.

Fig. 1.2. Combat scene with solar disc.
Old Sun Inn, Saffron Walden, Essex.

Archaic buildings, too, were circular, from the bender tents of nomads and the stone-and-wood homes of the ancient Celts to the traditional makeshift shelters of forest charcoal burners, which were made until the early twentieth century (Pennick 2006b, 96–97). The oldest structures by far in Great Britain are circular—the megalithic stone circles. To the Etruscans, from whom the Western geomantic tradition, the Etruscan discipline, largely comes, circular temples were dedicated to a single deity, while rectangular ones served any trinity of gods (Fergusson 1893, 292). At the time of Plato, unlike in Egypt, where Amun-Ra, the sun god, was the supreme deity, Greek religion did not give a very important role to the sun as a god. But with growing Egyptian and Persian influence, Helios (the Roman Sol) increased in importance as the years went by, and in Hellenistic times, he was seen as the ruling deity, Helios Pantokrator. A Hellenistic prayer to Helios addresses him: "All-ruler, spirit of the world, power of the world, light of the world" (Cumont 1919, 322). The physical sun was seen to possess a spiritual dimension, the Intelligible Helios. In the third century CE, Elagabalus, a Syrian sun worshipper, became emperor and renamed himself Heliogabalus (reign 222–226 CE). He instituted the worship at Rome of the Syrian solar deity El Gabel. In 274 CE, after an epiphany of the sun god appeared to his army, the Emperor Aurelian proclaimed Sol Invictus, the unvanquished sun, as the supreme god of the Empire (Warde-Fowler 1911, lecture 6, 118ff; Usener 1905, 465ff; Laing 1931, 150–53). Images of Sol Invictus show him with his right hand raised in benediction and with an orb, whip, or thunderbolt in his left (Usener 1905, 470ff). Mithras, too, was identified with the sun god; inscriptions dedicated to him were "to the Invincible Sun Mithras" (Laing 1931, 144). The Christian church took over the pagan view of the sun god as the spiritual light of the world. In place of the unconquered sun, Sol Invictus, Christ was declared the sun of righteousness, Sol Iustitiae, the judge of mankind (Usener 1905, 480). Jesus took on the judgmental attribute of the Babylonian sun god Shamash, with the biblical justification from the Jewish prophet Malachi, "But unto you that fear my Name shall the sun of righteousness arise" (Malachi 4:2), an essentially legalistic, contractual view of the nature of religious devotion.

Fig. I.3. Minoan gold sun wheel, Crete, circa 1600 BCE

The biblical sun became the new interpretation of the old supreme imperial god, Sol Invictus. The birth of Jesus was celebrated on December 25, the birthday of the son of Helios, Mithras (Usener 1905, 465; Laing 1931, 143–49). The solar attributes of light that illuminate all hidden things are attached to the concept of the all-seeing eye of God and through that to the Last Judgment. The fifteenth-century commentator Petrus Berchorius tells us, "Further I say of this Sun that he shall be inflamed when he sits in judgment. . . . For as the sun, when in the center of his orbit, that is to say the midday point, is hottest, so shall Christ be when he shall appear in the center of heaven and earth, that is to say, in Judgment" (Berchorius, 1489/1499). The Christ, as Sol Iustitiae, the Sun of Justice, is depicted at the central point, *medium coeli et terrae,* the location of the Throne of Majesty where he sits at the Last Judgment.

The cosmological symbolism of this solar throne is depicted in several medieval drawings. William Richard Lethaby describes a thirteenth-century manuscript at Heidelberg that showed "the Throne of Majesty standing on seven decreasing circular steps forming to the earth the vaults of heaven." This had around it the inscription "seven steps in fashion of a hollow vault" (Lethaby 1891, 138). This is the ancient cosmology where the Earth, the central point, is overlaid by the seven planetary spheres. In the fourth century CE, the Emperor Constantine adopted the basilica as the form for the Christian place of worship, and this was also the form of the Roman magisterial hall or courthouse where justice was meted out. The presiding judge sat on a throne raised on steps set in an apse. Churches were built in which the judicial apse became the sanctuary containing the altar, orientated axially east-west in accordance with sunrise, with the interior use of sunlight as a significant consideration (Pennick 1979a, 103–9; Pennick

2005b, 24–27; Pennick 2006d, 112–16). In the fifth century CE, Pope Leo complained that in Rome worshippers in St. Peter's turned away from the altar and faced the door to adore the rising sun (Laing 1931, 192). The major early churches of Rome were orientated with the altar in the west, but in the fifth century, orientation was altered for new churches so that the altar was located in the east. Central to the domes of Byzantine churches and many rose windows is the figure of Christ as Helios Pantokrator, sometimes in a solar aureole, or if the ornamentation of the church was made during a period when images were forbidden, a cross was substituted for the human figure.

The meaning of glyphs is notoriously fluid. Sheila Paine, a prolific collector of symbolic objects, lists the rayed sun, swastika, whorl, rosette, stars with four or eight points, cross in circle, ax, apple, lotus flower, cock, and scarab as solar symbols used as amulets (Paine 2004, 134). The cross as a symbol of the sun long predates Christian symbolism. It appears sometimes in the sky as a natural phenomenon in the regions approaching the terrestrial poles. Under certain conditions, sunlight or moonlight seen through airborne ice crystals creates halos. The patterns produced have a series of related forms, shown in figure 1.4.

These patterns include a pillar of light and "mock suns" (sun dogs) flanking the sun itself, sometimes linked by lines of light and making a cross in a circle of light. Outside the sun wheel may be other arcs (Pennick 1997a, 24–26). These solar wheel patterns are a very impressive phenomenon, bringing a sense of awe to the person who sees one.

Fig. 1.4. Observed sun-wheel phenomena, all possibilities shown together. Drawing by the author.

Clearly, the pattern can be perceived as an ostentum (a technical term from the Etruscan Discipline), of the divine power of the sun. There are many Bronze Age rock carvings in northern Europe in the form of the quartered circle or sun wheel, and it is probable that they refer to the solar phenomenon. Some of the rock art at Bohuslän, Östfold, and Östergötland in Scandinavia, depicts such wheels, which are ascribed to the sun by modern commentators (Gelling and Davidson 1971, 9–26).

Some carvings are clearly the wheels of chariots, but others appear to be objects carried by human figures. This wheel-cross pattern was adopted later by Christians of the Celtic church and became known as the Celtic cross. An early form of it on a stone at St. Dogmaels, Wales, is shown in figure 1.5.

Carl G. Jung saw the cross-in-a-circle as an archetype of wholeness, the sun wheel being the outer symbol of an inner image, and Edred Thorsson places it under the "quadraplectic signs" that symbolize the sky, sun, and lightning (Jung 1964, 241–42; Thorsson 1993, 14). Signs

Fig. 1.5. Stone carved with sun-wheel cross, probably eighth century, St. Dogmaels, Wales.

like this appear in Europe in the crafts of metalworking and wood-working from early times. The glyph was used by the ancient Germanic handworkers, as in the design of the metal fittings from Allemannic graves. Ceremonial bread baked in Germany, possibly an unbroken Allemannic tradition, takes the form of the sun wheel, often stamped with crosses. Certain timber-frame buildings in England and Germany bear the glyph as an integral part of the construction, as in the Royal Oak Inn at Tenbury. The glyph was used by metal founders in cast-ing ventilation grilles for early glazed windows, as in the Elizabethan House in Great Yarmouth. But few such remain in existence.

The sacred pillar called Irminsul that was venerated by the Saxons was destroyed by order of the Emperor Charlemagne in 772 CE. Its form, reconstructed from images in manuscripts and by extrapolation from the carving on the Externsteine rock formation, has roots both in the solar flared V pattern appearing in rock art and in representations of the world tree in Babylonian art (Pennick 1997a, 58–60). An image of Irminsul is shown in figure 1.6.

Fig. 1.6. Irminsul as it is portrayed now

Whatever its actual form in the eighth century, this is how Irminsul is perceived today. The sun symbolically related to a doorway appeared as long ago as the trilithons of Stonehenge. In ancient flat-Earth cosmol-ogies, the rising and setting points of the sun were viewed as doors in the sky through which the sun entered and left the Earth each day. The Gate of the East admitted the sun, and the Gate of the West allowed it to depart. At night it traveled through the dark path of the underworld.

Fig. 1.7. Cast sun-wheel ventilators from a sixteenth-century window, Great Yarmouth, Norfolk

Fig. 1.8. Sun over eighteenth-century door, Heidelberg, Germany

A solar emblem above a door signifies the triumph of light over darkness. An ancient Egyptian inscription at Edfu describes the triumph of the solar hero Horus over Set, lord of darkness. In memory of this victory, Thoth, god of writing and records, decreed that the solar emblem should be depicted over every door in Egypt. Figure 1.8 shows a sun over a seventeenth-century door in Heidelberg, Germany.

Fig. 1.10.
Colored-glass fanlight,
nineteenth century, Leicester

Fig. 1.11.
Cartoon by Andrew Stoddart,
Fig. 1.9. Sunburst fanlight,   1903, for a leaded-glass window.
St. John, Smith Square, London   The Library of the European Tradition.

Windows above the door, the fanlight, are often semicircular in form, with the window panels arranged as a sunburst or rayed sun, as shown in figure 1.9, in St. John's Church, Smith Square, London (architect Thomas Archer, built 1714–1728). The nineteenth-century glass-in-lead window in Leicester illustrated in figure 1.10 overtly has the form of the sun with its solar flares.

The pattern was popular in Arts and Crafts–inspired suburban housing of the first part of the twentieth century, and in contemporary white plastic front doors it appears integrally as the dropped fanlight. In figure 1.11 a 1903 sketch by Andrew Stoddart for such a window shows us an early example of the genre, with the flying birds motif that appears in the work of the Arts and Crafts architect Baillie Scott.

Fig. 1.12. Sunburst motif on radiator of 1920s Albion Motors truck

The pattern also appeared on an Albion Motors truck of the 1920s, in its trademarked glyph claiming its reliability "as sure as the sunrise" (fig. 1.12) (Brown 1982, 8, 10). The sunburst pattern in East Anglian pargeting is different from the rayed sun glyph, being concentric part rings made with a stamp that allows a tessellated pattern to be made on the plastered wall.

The apparent motion of the sun is used for telling time with sundials. The sundial shows us the place we are on Earth as well as the time we are in, because its geometry is defined by its latitude. It is always in harmony with the conditions, unlike our general use of mechanical time telling, which dislocates us from the passing of the day. "It is better to travel hopefully than to arrive," the motto on an early twentieth-century dial at Hunstanton, Norfolk, tells us, while the hourglasses beside it warn us that our time is not long (fig. 1.13).

Fig. 1.13. Sundial, 1908, New Hunstanton, Norfolk, with hourglass glyphs and the motto "It is better to travel hopefully than to arrive." The designer of the sundial was Herbert Ibberson.

Fig. 1.14. Traditional sun-wheel bread, southern Germany

Fig. 1.15. The Royal Oak Inn at Tenbury, showing sun-wheel patterns integral with the timber-frame structure

2. THE AKHET AND THE TWIN TOWERS

Solar symbolism is deeply embedded in Western culture on a larger scale than just fanlight design. Richard H. Wilkinson points out that in ancient Egyptian culture the forms of many hieroglyphs were reproduced as actual objects. Glyphs were employed in the design of various artifacts, and natural objects were viewed as embodiments of the hieroglyph. Thus, for instance, the headrest from the tomb of Tutankhamen reflects the form of the *akhet,* the hieroglyph signifying the point of the rising and setting of the sun on the horizon.

Fig. 2.1. The Egyptian *akhet* glyph, which represents the sun on the horizon between hills

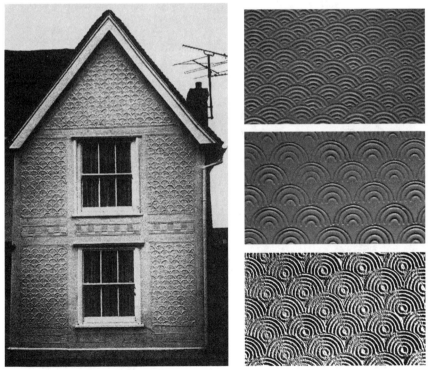

Fig. 2.2. Pargeted sunbursts: left, Great Chesterford; top right, Thaxted, Essex; middle right, Ashdon, Essex; lower right, Saffron Walden, Essex

The pylons of Egyptian temples form part of the akhet, and when the sun rises on the temple axis, the whole glyph is present in physical form (Wilkinson 1994, 166–67). An inscription on the Temple of Ptah at Memphis tells us, "Its gates are like the heavenly horizon of light" (Lethaby 1891, 178). The horns of consecration at Knossos on Crete also take this form.

Influential in Christian architecture are the porchway pillars of the Jewish temple in Jerusalem, constructed on the orders of King Solomon as recorded in the Bible (1 Kings 6:1–38; 7:15–22). Derived from the obelisks flanking Egyptian temples were two metal castings, pillars called Boaz and Jachin (fig. 2.3). They were cast by the Phoenician craftsman Hiram and are customarily said to be hollow as repositories for sacred writings. The pillar Boaz was named after the great-grandfather of King David, and Jewish kings after Solomon were crowned at the foot of one of the pillars. The meaning of the pillars' names, according to Masonic traditions, are Boaz, "in it strength," and Jachin, "he will make firm" or "he

Fig. 2.3. Left: Engraving of the columns Boaz and Jachin at the Jewish temple, John Sturt, London, 1721, during the formative period of speculative Freemasonry; right: entrance gate pillars in Boaz and Jachin at the Royal Naval Hospital, Greenwich, designed by Thomas Ripley, 1751

will establish," interpreted as "He in whom strength is, may he establish [this house]" (Jones 1956, 358–59).

Twin towers were a feature of major churches from the Romanesque period onward, and in the Gothic period, some magnificent structures were designed and built. The twin towers of All Souls College in Oxford, designed by Nicholas Hawksmoor and built 1708–1730, are illustrated in figure 2.4.

The famous twin towers at the western entrance of Westminster Abbey are also Hawksmoor's designs. In the twentieth century, the national football stadium of England, Wembley, was known as the Twin Towers from its construction for the Empire Exhibition in 1923 until its demolition. Now that the towers at Wembley are gone, the name Twin Towers evokes images of the former World Trade Center in New York, destroyed in 2001.

Fig. 2.4. Twin towers in the north quadrangle of All Souls College, Oxford. Designed by Nicholas Hawksmoor, built 1708–1730.

3. THE EIGHT-SPOKED WHEEL

The rose of the winds is familiar from mariners' compasses that are in the form of a circle divided into the four cardinal directions: north, east, south, and west, subdivided into eight by the intercardinal directions, and then further subdivided into sixteen and thirty-two (figs. 3.1 and 3.2). At any particular place the characteristic weather of the corresponding direction can be noted, and the rose of the winds is a useful rule of thumb.

Fig. 3.1. The eightfold wheel

Fig. 3.2. The eightfold star

The rune *wyn* is in the form of a weather vane, like those known to have been set on Viking ships as well as on the temples and stave churches of Scandinavia (fig. 3.3). *Wyn* signifies joy, that elusive state of being that is harmony within the chaos of the world. Joy is gained by being in accepting balance with external events, just as the weather vane moves in accordance with the prevailing current of air, yet remains stable in its position (Pennick 1992b, 74–75; 1999b, 53, 75).

Fig. 3.3. *Wyn* rune

The eightfold wheel and the star with eight arms signify the eight winds that were formalized in the Mediterranean in ancient times and recorded in the influential architectural writings of Vitruvius. This eightfold division is symbolized in the octagonal form of any tower that is orientated to the cardinal and intercardinal directions and bearing a weather vane (Pennick 1999a, 140–61; Pennick 2005b, 124–28). In northern Europe the cardinal directions are symbolized by four dwarfs: Nordri, Ostri, Sudri, and Vestri, who support the canopy of heaven. In Amsterdam the iconic Amsterdamse School-style building Het Scheepvaarthuis (built 1913–1916 by architect Melchior van der Mey) has representations of these dwarfs. The brick ceiling of the main entrance has a light fixture that represents the constellation of the Great Bear. This is framed by an octagon inside a square whose northern corner is a lamp signifying the Pole Star. The four sides of the square are supported by the four dwarfs (Boeterenbrood and Prang 1989, 101, fig. 81).

According to Herman Wirth, traditionally the eightfold wheel was one of the signs for the year—the old Norse *eyktamark* or *dagsmark*—signifying the eight *aettir,* the directions or points on the horizon in the "arctic-north Atlantic year-division" (Wirth 1931–1936, vol. 1, 85; vol. 2, 155). The eightfold division in the north is best known from Scandinavia, the Faroe Islands, the Shetland Islands, and Iceland (Pennick 1990c, 76–87; Pennick 1999a, 123–24). The system of the division of the horizon into eight sections applies to place, space, and time (fig. 3.4).

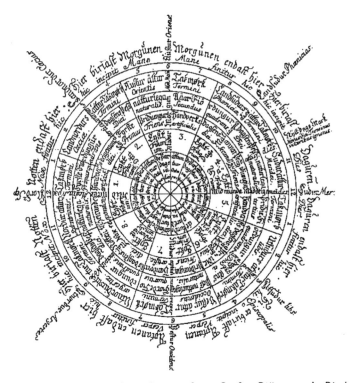

Fig. 3.4. Rose of the winds and time, from Stefan Björnsson's *Rimbegla*, Copenhagen, 1780. The Library of the European Tradition.

The word *aett* (Scots airt and Irish aird) means a group of eight, as in the three aettir of the runes; a region of the sky; a specific one of the eight directions, cardinal and intercardinal; a homestead; and even a family. Thus place, space, time, and human descent are integrated. The day-and-night cycle is also divided into eight tides, determined from the sun's position above or below the horizon. Each tide, three hours in modern reckoning, occupies one aett of the horizon circle. Figure 3.5 shows the directions and their corresponding tides of the day.

The eightfold division of the day into tides was extended to the whole year-circle, dividing it into eight sacred festivals. The antiquity of this eight-festival year is disputed. For a brief overview of the *four* festivals of the Celtic year, see Hutton (1996, 408–11). After World War II, this eightfold year was popularized in Anglo-American paganism as the Eight Festivals (e.g., Alex Sanders's witches' calendar [Johns 1969, 142–44]), and now it is a significant characteristic of contemporary pagan practices. A possible influence on this development may be that the eightfold wheel has long been a symbol of the Buddhist eightfold path, and in Taoism, part of the talisman of the Messenger of the Nine Heavens is an eight-spoked wheel of fire (Legeza 1975, 9).

The Catherine wheel is an eight-spoked wheel with spikes, a symbol of the martyrdom of the Christian saint Catherine of Alexandria,

Fig. 3.5. Rune wheel showing the hours of the day and night, the eight tides of the day, and the directions. Diagram by the author, 1991.

the earliest woman to be called a virgin martyr. Like many iconic religious individuals, there is no historical record of St. Catherine being tortured on a spiky wheel for refusing the state duty of worshipping the gods. The wheel that is her symbol is said to have broken, and subsequently she was beheaded. Her image shows her holding a wheel in the same manner as the icons of Fortuna, Saturn, Arianrhod, Krodo, and other deities who rule over aspects of time. A 1492 engraving of the Central European god Krodo in Bothe's *Chroneken der Sassen* reproduced in figure 3.6 shows him holding a bucket and a six-spoked flower like wheel (Franz 1943, 35–39, 83). As the god of time, Krodo has the attributes of Kronos-Saturn, whose attributes are the eternal wheel of time and the scythe, which forms his sigil. But as a female figure, Catherine is most close to the goddess of fortune, Fortuna, "the goddess who brings," whose Roman festival was celebrated at the summer solstice (Laing 1931, 98). Her wheel was not viewed as a symbol of instability and fickleness, however, but as a representation of the orb of the sun (Laing 1931, 101). The custom of rolling a wheel downhill at midsummer, sometimes a literal wheel of fire, is associated with some midsummer bonfires, such as on St. John's Eve (Franklin 2002, 28).

Fig. 3.6. The Central European god of time, Krodo, from Bothe's *Chroneken der Sassen,* 1492. The Library of the European Tradition.

Fortuna continues in popular consciousness in contemporary times as Lady Luck, whose "wheel of fortune" is celebrated in the tarot trump number ten and in actual gambling in the form of mechanical wheels of fortune, including roulette, twister, and various forms of television gambling and state lotteries (Pennick 2006b, 163). Traditional in Breton churches were wheels with bells around the rim. They were turned by sick people in the hope of effecting a cure (Baring-Gould 1901, 198–99; Johnston 1912, 202). Buddhist prayer wheels express the same principle. The wheel remains the emblem of St. Catherine's College in Cambridge. In medieval England this wheel was the sign of the Worshipful Company of Turners. As an inn sign, it was altered sometimes to the Cat and Wheel or the Clock Wheel (Monson-Fitzjohn 1926, 43). The Catherine wheel gave its name to a particular kind of firework that rotates around a pin hammered into a wooden post or tree. Hanging an old cartwheel on the outer wall of a building is a tradition in parts of northern Europe, the spokes standing for the rays of the sun. The runic correspondence of the wheel is *rad,* signifying motion and the vehicle that allows us to progress, channeling our energies in effective ways. In the runes it is not necessarily an eightfold wheel that is meant, but the principle of the wheel, as traditional wheelwrights tended to make ten-spoked wheels that were geometrically stronger.

4. CROSSES

The sun wheel contains the cross, and it is with the sun that the cross was connected until it was adopted widely as a Christian symbol representing the doctrines of vicarious atonement and redemption. Because Jesus was crucified, it became a central emblem of the religion, though the connection between a wooden cross as a form of execution and the solar cross is fortuitous. However, the incorporation of a large body of divine solar lore into Christian symbology meant that the previous uses and meanings of the cross were also appropriated. The Egyptian sacred glyph, the *ankh,* signifying the sun on the horizon, was assimilated into the same milieu. This image is a visible part of life on Earth and cannot

Fig. 4.2. The ankh (round form)

Fig. 4.3. The ankh (elongated form)

Fig. 4.4. Chi-Rho

Fig. 4.1. Equinoctial sunset,
Lake Garda, Italy

be eliminated as a non-Christian symbol, as shown in figures 4.1, 4.2, and 4.3 by an equinoctial sunset and two ankhs.

During a long period—nearly the first half of the religion's existence so far—the cross did not have the preeminence that it later attained as an almost exclusively Christian glyph. That happened from the ninth century onward (Whittick 1971, 224–25). The swastika, a stylized fish, the grapevine, the sixfold Chrismon, and the Greek letters *alpha* and *omega* were all emblematic of the faith and its doctrines. The Chi-Rho, a monogram composed of the Greek characters *chi* and *rho,* was a major contender as the primal Christian glyph before the cross gained ascendancy (fig. 4.4).

Fig. 4.5. Greek (equal-armed) cross

Fig. 4.6. Floriated cross by Augustus Welby Pugin, 1868. The Library of the European Tradition

Fig. 4.7. Blacksmith-made door handle with cross door plate, Hereford

Fig. 4.8. Pargeted crosses, Great Waltham, Essex

Because crosses can be drawn with equal or unequal arms, the two main sects of Christianity, Eastern Orthodoxy and Roman Catholicism, have two different crosses associated with them. The Orthodox cross is equilateral and is called the Greek cross because of its churchly associations (fig. 4.5).

The cross with one long arm is called the Latin cross. This cross lends itself to embellishment and ornamentation, as shown by the illustration in figure 4.6, from the nineteenth-century master of Gothic architecture Augustus Welby Pugin.

This cross is used as a magical sigil of protection, as in the traditional blacksmith-made door fitting in Hereford (fig. 4.7) and the pargeting work on a house in Great Waltham, Essex (fig. 4.8).

As an identifying sign where Christian identity is significant, the cross is used as a tattoo. A picture from around 1890 shows a young Christian woman in Bosnia, tattooed as a spiritual sign that would also prevent her from being forcibly converted to the Mohammedan religion (fig. 4.9).

Fig. 4.9. Young woman with Christian tattoos to prevent forcible conversion to the Muslim religion, Bosnia, circa 1890. The Library of the European Tradition.

The tau cross, which is the character *T* when used in writing, is called after the Greek name for that letter. Another name is the gibbet cross (Whittick 1971, 224). Associated with St. Anthony of Egypt, who is depicted with a tau cross as a staff, along with his sacred pig and bell, some see the *tau* as a glyph signifying the tree of life, representing fecundity and vibrant life. St. Anthony lived in ancient tombs and conjured up the ancient Egyptian gods in order to struggle with them, an image familiar from illustrations of the temptation of St. Anthony. So the tau cross is also a sigil of magical protection against powerful hostile spiritual forces that one has called up, a function of all kinds of crosses in the Christian context.

Crosses as European military honors have their origin in medieval orders of knighthood. The emergence of heraldry in the twelfth century led to the cross being adopted as a sign of Christian knights on duty defending the Christian lands of the Byzantine Empire against Muslim invaders. Attempts to recapture the Holy Land from occupying Saracen forces led crusaders who spoke different languages to adopt various colored crosses as a form of identification. Thus English-speakers had a red cross and Germans a black cross, both on a white field. Danes had a white cross on a red field, Swedes a yellow cross on a blue field. The present flags of some of these nations come from this time. The cross of St. George, a red cross on a white field, is the flag of England and appears in representations of the national spiritual guardian. The stained-glass image of St. George and the dragon that I made in 2006 is shown in figure 4.10.

Various independent orders of knighthood had their own forms of cross. The hilt of the sword is in the form of a cross, and this, too, played a symbolic part in Christian chivalry, later appearing in war memorials combined with a wreath to form a Celtic cross (fig. 4.11).

Fig. 4.10. Stained-glass image of St. George and the dragon, made by the author, 2006

Fig. 4.11. Sword and wreath as sun wheel. Italy, early twentieth century. The Library of the European Tradition.

The crusading Knights of St. John (the Knights Hospitaller) became the masters of Malta, and their cross is the Maltese cross (fig. 4.12). In the nineteenth century, some of these crosses were recalled in new military medals.

Fig. 4.12. Cross of the Knights of St. John (Maltese cross). The Library of the European Tradition.

The iconic German military decoration, Das Eiserne Kreuz (the Iron Cross), was instituted by King Frederick III of Prussia in 1813 and reestablished for subsequent wars (Franco-Prussian War, 1870; World War I, 1914; World War II, 1939) (Hieronymussen and Strüwing 1967, 171–72). The Iron Cross's form and color—iron and silver, black and white—follows the escutcheon of Der Deutsche Ritterorden, the Teutonic Order of Knighthood, which in the middle ages fought a series of crusades against the pagans in Old Prussia, Pomerania, Kurland, Riga, Semgallia, Livonia, Wierland, and other tribal areas in the Baltic lands on the borders of Russia (now parts of Germany, Poland, Lithuania, and Latvia). The knights established a Christian military state, the Ordensstaat, which was at its maximum extent in the early fifteenth century. A World War II Iron Cross is illustrated in figure 4.13. The Nazis substituted a swastika for the original oak leaves at the center of the cross.

Fig. 4.13. Iron Cross, 1939 issue with swastika. Iron and silver. Author's collection.

The highest British military honor is the Victoria Cross, instituted by Queen Victoria in 1856 at the behest of Prince Albert, in emulation of the Iron Cross. Victoria Crosses are made in bronze from cannons captured from the Russian army during the Crimean War. From the use of the cross as a medical glyph by the Knights of St. John, the Red Cross for medical aid is ultimately derived, and from that, as the red cross is fiercely guarded by the organization, the green cross is used to indicate medical emergency packages and pharmacies, though for a short time the green cross was also used in a road-safety campaign. The Blue Cross, derived from these forerunners, is an organization in the United Kingdom that looks after pets (and with a blue shield, a commercial health insurance company for people in the United States), and the black cross is an anarchist sign of mutual aid and prisoner support.

5. THE CRESCENT MOON, STAR, AND COMET

We know by the moon
That we are not too soon
And we know by the sky
That we are not too high
We know by the star
That we are not too far
And we know by the ground
That we are within sound.

THE GOWER WASSAIL

Apart from being the night light of the Earth, the moon is a recognizable measure of the passing of time. Unlike the sun, which always appears the same, the moon changes continually, and in some cosmologies it is not a single moon lit by the sun from different apparent angles that we see, but a succession of moons, each arising anew after the old one has gone, hence the expression "new moon." We sometimes say figuratively that many moons have passed since something happened, and the calendar is divided into months (moonths) that no longer are defined by the lunar, but by the solar year. A different cultural perception is that the moon has a cycle, and in this it is likened to a woman's monthly cycle. The tides of the sea rise and fall according to the phases of the moon, and the same influence is deemed to affect the human body. During its waxing and waning phases, the moon is crescentic. The crescent and star formed the glyph of

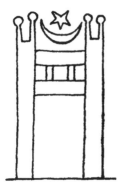

Fig. 5.1. Propylon of the Temple of
Aphrodite at Paphos, Cyprus, with
the goddess's crescent-and-star
glyph. Drawing by William Richard
Lethaby from a coin. The Library
of the European Tradition.

the goddess Aphrodite, which was later adopted as a Muslim glyph and
is present today on the flags of some countries. Similar Etruscan glyphs
show the crescent with a smaller disc where the star is, as in the Cypriot
example shown in figure 5.1 (Petrie 1930, XXVII, G2). This drawing,
by William Richard Lethaby from an ancient Cypriot coin from Paphos,
shows the glyph above a sacred propylon (Lethaby 1891, 183).

As a glyph the disc of the full moon is indistinguishable from the
disc of the sun unless it is colored, when the moon is silver-white and
the sun is red. Frederick Thomas Elworthy in *The Evil Eye* put forward
the idea that the crescent was used as an amulet to attract the eye of the
malevolent and thus deflect its baleful influence away from the wearer
(Elworthy 1895, 202). Thus horns were worn as amulets. Crescents
made from wolves' teeth and boars' tusks were used as ancient British
amulets, and in traditional clothing shops in Bavaria today, one can pur-
chase *Wendeketten,* chains of amulets hung with curved tusks and teeth.
In Elworthy's day horns in the form of crescents were common on horse
trappings in Italy (Elworthy 1895, 204), and English horse brasses have
the crescent among myriad other glyphs. In the early part of the twentieth century, Lina Eckenstein made a collection of old horse brasses and
asserted that their designs were ancient ones that had been in continuous use until her day (Brears 1981, 43). She saw the crescent as a lunar
symbol. In India and southern Europe, the horns of the crescent were
always pointed downward, she wrote, but in the north, they pointed
upward. Eckenstein found such horned crescents of Roman date from
Suffolk and Norfolk and took this as a sign of direct continuity. Later
British horse brass researchers traced their history and found that they

date from the eighteenth century (Brears 1981, 44). But of course, the use of glyphs always transfers from one medium to another, as all the illustrations printed in this book prove, so the continuity of the use of the glyph cannot be discounted so easily. There is a generic relationship in form between the crescent moon, the horn, the horseshoe, and the sickle (Von Zaborsky 1936, 74–79).

Fig. 5.2. Star Wheel. Gustav Wolf, 1922.
The Library of the European Tradition.

The stars are the basis for astrology, being the fixed background on which the planets appear to wander. In a Christian context, the single star refers to the story of the birth of Jesus, when the Magi were led to seek out his birthplace because they saw a significant star. The rubric "I am a star that goes with thee and shines out of the depths" is attributed to the Mithraic tradition (Butler 1975, 172). Seen as a sign from God, the Star of Bethlehem amalgamates with the mariners' use of the North Star, otherwise known as the lode star and the nail, and called Polaris in present-day astronomical terminology. This star, which in the last millennia has appeared to stand above the terrestrial pole, was a guiding

light for those navigating at sea and on land. This is shown conventionally as a six-pointed glyph, which has a similar form to the hexflower,
but with a different meaning.

Among the other quite different interpretations of her divine
nature, Our Lady is shown in Christian iconography as the queen of
heaven. She is clad in vestments bearing stars that link her allegori-
cally with the birth story of Jesus as well as absorbing the attributes
of the ancient Egyptian goddess Nuit. Commentators on the tarot
trump the star also link it with the Egyptian goddess Nuit (e.g., Suster
1990, 50), though the Egyptian connection is a late addition to the
tarot mythos. The star as a tarot card has the traditional imagery of a
woman with vases in each hand, an image of one of the four cardinal
virtues, Temperance, who pours water into wine, producing a synthesis
that retains the best qualities of two opposites while eliminating their
worst natures (Pennick and Field 2004, 94). Temperance is the quality of the middle way between reason and desire. The sun, moon, and
star are shown in figure 5.3 in an alchemical engraving from *Rosarium
Philosophorum* (published in Frankfurt, Germany, in 1550), where the
sun is depicted with a king, the moon with a queen, and the star with a
crested bird that mediates between the two opposites.

Fig. 5.3. The sun-king,
moon-queen, and star-bird.
The Library of the European
Tradition.

The rune *tir* (*teiwaz*) signified the ancient Germanic god of the sky, Tîwaz, whom the Old English called Tiw and the Norse, Tyr. It is a glyph that signified order and its maintenance. The oldest extant text describing the meaning of the runes, *The Old English Rune Poem,* tells us, "*Tir* is a special sign. It keeps faith well with princes, it is always on course in the darkness of night; it never fails." This is a description of the star Tir, always visible at night over the North Pole. In its form Tir is the arrow that points the way, at least to modern eyes. Whether as a star Tir meant the pole star, the nail, or nave of the wheel of the heavens, the guiding light of navigators, is not certain. In heraldry a version of this glyph was depicted as "a missile instrument with a barbed head thrown from a cross bow," known as the pheon. From this, by simplification, the British government broad arrow is said to stem. The Broad Arrow was a heraldic sign called the Pheon, which the British government adopted as a mark for its property. Figure 5.4 shows a broad arrow from a British military plan of 1877, and figure 5.5 shows the same sign cast in a cannon of 1840.

The same glyph can be viewed as signifying three equal lines descending as rays of light from above (fig. 5.6), and in this form it is the Welsh Awen, Yr Arwydd Glan (the Sacred Symbol), the creative name of God (*Ab Ithel* 1867, vol. 1, xl).

Fig. 5.4. British War Department broad arrow, 1877

Fig. 5.5. Cannon, Harwich, Essex, dated 1840 and marked with the British War Department broad arrow

Fig. 5.6. The Tir rune

Generally, the rune is symbolic of cosmic consciousness. The symbolic meaning of Yr Arwydd Glan is given in *Barddas:* "They are called the three columns, and the three columns of truth, because there can be no knowledge of the truth, but from the light thrown upon it" (Ab Ithel 1867, I, 67) (fig. 5.7). Bardic tradition tells that these three lines were the primary signs from which all ancient British writing was derived (Ab Ithel 1867, I, 50–53, 68–69).

Fig. 5.7. Druidic sigil with spirals and Awen. *The Golden Section Order,* 1983. The Library of the European Tradition.

Like the meteor, or a falling star that is said to denote the death of someone, comets are portentous omen, taken to presage disaster and doom. Comets are rarely depicted outside actual records of them, as in the Bayeux Tapestry.

Weather vanes in the form of comets are few, but some were set up in eighteenth-century London on Sir Christopher Wren's Church of St. Mary Aldermanbury and James Gibbs's St. Mary-le-Strand. Another comet vane, designed in 1727 by Nicholas Hawksmoor and John James, topped the Church of St. John, Horselydown, London, which was bombed in World War II and demolished as late as 1970 (fig. 5.8).

Fig. 5.8. Comet weather vane formerly on the apex of the columnar steeple of the Church of St. John, Horselydown, London, designed by Nicholas Hawksmoor and John James, and destroyed in 1970. Drawing by Charles G. Harper, 1923. The Library of the European Tradition.

In 1931 Cecil Parker described the Church of St. John as "one of those queer eighteenth-century churches which seem to have been the especial feature of that rather pagan era" (Harper 1931, 238–39). A comet vane was also planned for one of Gibbs's London churches, St. Martin-in-the-Fields (completed in 1726), but it was not installed (Pennick 2005b, 169–76).

6. SOLAR LIGHT AND LIGHTNING

The rune *sigel* (fig. 6.1) signifies the power of the sun, not a flash of lightning. The Roman thunderbolt of Jupiter was portrayed surrounded by a number of arrow-pointed lightning flashes, never as a single flash.

Fig. 6.1. Sigel rune

It is the rune that resists darkness and dissolution, death and disintegration, a rune of hope in *The Old English Rune Poem* that leads one out of dangerous situations. During the first half of the twentieth century, the similarity of Guido List's Armanen rune name *sig* to the German word *Seig* (victory) was one reason for its use by the Nazis in the emblems of the Schutzstaffel (SS) and various youth organizations of that period (fig. 6.2).

Fig. 6.2. Logo of the Nazi SS

At the same time the lightning flash was used as a logo by Sir Oswald Mosley's British Union of Fascists, founded in 1932 (Shermer 1971, 55), later renamed the Union Movement. A 1957 example of the Union logo is shown in figure 6.3.

Fig. 6.3. The British Union of Fascists' glyph in the word
Union, 1957. The Library of the European Tradition.

Toward the end of Mosley's organization, the flash was given an arrow-head, becoming an inverted form of the thunderbolt rune *ziu* (Pennick 1999b, 77). This has been a very popular glyph, used to signify a number of different meanings: as the logo of various electrical companies, as a warning sign of overhead electric wires on trains, as a badge for military signals officers in the East German Army, and by the West German squatter movement from the 1960s as a sign that an empty building had been commandeered and occupied (fig. 6.4).

Fig. 6.4. The lightning/electricity/
communications/occupation glyph

Later this glyph was used with fascist imagery as the logo of the provocative singer Marilyn Manson. It is yet another instance of a single glyph bearing many different interpretations, depending entirely on the context in which it is used. Another version of the glyph, designed in the 1960s by Gerald Barney for the British Railways Board, was said to combine the meaning of two-way traffic and the flash of electrification (fig. 6.5).

Fig. 6.5. British Railways glyph signifying both two-way traffic and
rails with an electrification flash. Designed by Gerald Barney of the
Design Research Unit, 1964. The Library of the European Tradition.

7. THE COSMIC OR PHILOSOPHICAL EGG

As the progenitor of the independent organism, the egg is a symbol of coming into being. It is the shape given to the omphalos that marks the navel of the Earth, a conceptual center point that mediates between the underworld, this world, and the upperworld in European geomancy. The human navel marks the place in the body where it was connected to the mother in the womb, and hence it is the origin point. The religion of Orpheus teaches that before time existed in the cosmos, when there was only chaos and night, the cosmic egg emerged and cracked open, and from that emerged the four elements of matter as well as time. The contemporary scientific interpretation of the breaking of the cosmic egg is the big bang theory. As Aristophanes wrote in his play *The Birds*:

> *At length, in the dreary chaotical closet*
> *Of Erebus old, was a secret deposit;*
> *By night the Primaeval in secrecy laid*
> *A Mystical Egg, that in silence and shade*
> *Was brooded and hatched.*
>   (LETHABY 1891, 263)

A Greek alchemical text, the *Anonymus,* expressing ideas current in the third and fourth centuries CE, places the origin of the four elements in this primordial cosmic egg of the philosophers, otherwise described as the seed of Pythagoras. This text's author expressed coming-into-being symbolism of the Orphic religion that appears in Aristophanes' play, and the image appeared much later in Europe in alchemical literature.

In his *Architecture: Mysticism and Myth* (1891), William Richard Lethaby described and explained the symbolic meaning of the elements of the eternal tradition in architecture. In chapter 12, "The Symbol of Creation," he tells of the symbolism of the cosmic egg as the progenitor of existence:

From desire and vapor proceeded primitive matter. It was a muddy water—black, icy, profound—encompassing insensible monsters, incoherent parts of forms to be born. Then matter condensed and became an egg. It broke; one half formed the earth and the other half the firmament. The sun, the moon, the winds, and the clouds appeared, and a crash of thunder awakened the sentient animals. (Lethaby 1891, 263)

The alchemical print of the cosmic egg illustrated in figure 7.1 comes from Heinrich Jamsthaler's 1625 work, *Viatorum Spagyricum*.

Lethaby notes that the egg, as a symbol of creation, has a connection with funeral rites, perhaps signifying rebirth or resurrection. He notes an antique pagan link between the egg and the dead. He states that "in a tomb at Bologna an Etruscan was exhumed with an egg in his hands," and quotes Eugène Dognée that "they affected the ovoid form of funeral vases" (Lethaby 1891, 267), and recalls Alfred Butler's comment that "marble eggs are said to have been discovered in some early martyrs' tombs at Rome, and that in all Christian lands eggs are associated with Eastertime, some think that the egg was regarded as emblematic of the Resurrection" (Lethaby 1891, 257). In pre-Christian sacred art and architecture, it was carved in the egg-and-dart moldings of the columns of the Ionic and Composite orders and in profile as the

Fig. 7.1. The alchemical cosmic egg, the Mateia Prima, with the emblems of the seven planets, male/female human, dragon, square and triangle (fourfold and threefold), and square and compass. Heinrich Jamsthaler, *Viatorum Spagyricum*, 1625. The Library of the European Tradition.

classical molding called the ovolo. The caryatids on the Erechtheum in Athens have headdresses composed of egg-and-dart garlands.

The London mystic William Blake wrote of the cosmic egg as the "mundane shell," where to him it signifies the outer limit of the physical universe. Blake's 1793 engraving *The Gates of Paradise* shows a winged putto emerging from a breaking egg. In *William Blake: Milton a Poem,* Blake's 1797 diagram of *The Four Zoas* (fig. 7.2) overlaps the cardinally directed spheres of Urthona, Luvah, Tharmas, and Urizen, and encompasses Adam and Satan (Essick and Viscomi 1998, 29). The "fires of Los" also burn within this "mundane shell." Blake's personal mythos is part of the ancient current of Hermetic science, for the *ovum philosophorum,* or philosophers' egg, is a fundamental component of the works of medieval and Renaissance philosophers. Like the urn and other hermetically sealed receptacles, the egg can symbolize the alchemical vessel within which transmutation is effected.

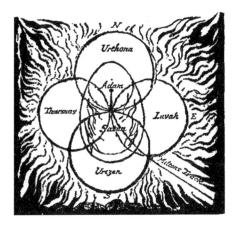

Fig. 7.2. William Blake, *The Four Zoas*, 1797. The Library of the European Tradition.

Nicolas Flamel (ca. 1330–ca. 1417), the French alchemist, described the egg's character in *Exposition of the Hieroglyphical Figures.* To Flamel the egg is just that—the vessel in which the philosophers' stone comes into being through manipulation of the four elements (Linden 2003, 132). The image of the cosmic egg appears in numerous alchemical works of the sixteenth and seventeenth centuries. It is on the title page of *Monas Hieroglyphica* (1564) by John Dee (1527–1606), which shows his emblematic *monas,* or hieroglyphic monad, as a sigil enclosed within an egg-shaped cartouche (Gettings 1981, 175) (see figure 31.4). Eggs are depicted as the

Fig. 7.3. Cosmic eggs, obelisks, dove-and-serpent weather vane, and sundials on The Gate of Honour, Gonville and Caius College, Cambridge, designed by Dr. John Caius and built in 1575. The Library of the European Tradition.

finials on either side of the engraving that makes a classical architectural setting for the text, the motif of the sacred gateway. In Cambridge the 1575 Gate of Honour at Gonville and Caius College, designed by Dr. John Caius (master of the college, 1559–1573), has obelisks at the four corners topped by cosmic eggs (Willis and Clark 1886, 1, 177–79). The finial is also a cosmic egg, once topped by a dove-and-serpent weather vane. A reconstruction by Willis and Clark is shown in figure 7.3.

Salomon Trismosin's late sixteenth-century *Splendor Solis* includes the cosmic egg, and *Emblema VIII* by Matthäus Merian in Michael Maier's alchemical work *Atalanta fugiens* (1617) depicts a philosopher wielding a sword, about to strike a large egg standing on a low table. The motto says, "Take the egg and cut it with a fiery sword." By smashing the egg, new elements of being will be released into existence. *Viatorum Spagyricum,* Heinrich Jamsthaler's 1625 hermetic work, depicts the "egg of nature" containing the seven traditional planets (the moon, Mercury, Venus, the sun, Mars, Jupiter, and Saturn), a dragon, a circle or sphere encompassing a triangle and square, and a human figure with both a man's and woman's head. This dual being holds a pair of compasses and a set square, which was later adopted as the symbol of freemasonry. In 1650 Thomas Vaughan likened the egg to the philosopher's stone or elixir in his *Coelum Terrae:*

I am the egg of Nature known only to the wise such as are pious and modest, who make of me a little world. Ordained I was by the Almighty God for men, but—though many desire me—I am given only to few that they may relieve the poor with my treasures and not set their minds on gold that perisheth. (Vaughan 1650)

The mundane egg is also an important element in Thomas Burnet's *Sacred Theory of the Earth* (1684–1690), which may have later influenced William Blake (Essick and Viscomi 1998, 29). The emblem book *Ova Paschialia Sacra Emblemata,* published in 1672 at Ingolstadt, Germany, deals with the spiritual oneness of the cosmic egg and the symbolic Easter egg. Illustrated in figures 7.4 and 7.5 are an Easter card from Belarus, with batik-on-fabric painting, and a well at Dürrbrunn, Bavaria, Germany, dressed at Eastertide with garlands and a cross egg.

In the seventeenth century, the cosmic egg was used in its own right as an architectural emblem on churches in the Netherlands. On

Fig. 7.4. Easter card with batik egg on fabric. Belarus, 1996. The Library of the European Tradition.

Fig. 7.5. Dressed well with garlands of Easter eggs and cross, Dürrbrunn, Bavaria, Germany

Fig. 7.6. Cosmic eggs atop
the facade of the Oostkerk
in Middelburg, Zeeland, the
Netherlands, (built 1648–1667)

the uppermost edges of the east front of the octagonal Oostkerk in
Middelburg (built 1648–1667), designed by Bartholomaeus Drijfhout
and Pieter Post, are cosmic eggs, garlanded like the omphalos of Delphi.
The Oostkerk eggs are illustrated in figure 7.6.

Similarly, the porch of the Nieuwe Kerk in the Hague (built 1649–
1656), designed by Pieter Noorwits and Barthold van Bassen, also has
garlanded eggs, a little different in form. An unbuilt plan by Nicholas
Hawksmoor for All Souls College, Oxford, has cosmic egg finials.
Robert Hooke, like Hawksmoor, an associate of Sir Christopher Wren,
had a drawing of the Nieuwe Kerk, and this may have been the source
of Hawksmoor's design (Whinney 1971, 64). Like the Dutch forerunners in Middelburg and the Hague, his cosmic eggs are garlanded.

According to Kerry Downes, the egg in this context symbolizes the
breaking of the bonds of death at the Last Judgment (Downes 1970,
78). The egg was recognized as such by the craftsmen who worked on
the classical churches in London after the Great Fire of 1666 (Pennick
2005b, 107–12). Through Lethaby symbolic eggs appeared in architecture in the Arts and Crafts movement at the end of the nineteenth
century. The Passmore Edwards Settlement at Tavistock Place, London,

was designed by two of Lethaby's disciples, Dunbar Smith (1866–1933) and Cecil Brewer (1871–1918), and built in 1897–1898. The main entrance, surmounted by egg finials, is illustrated in figure 7.7.

Fig. 7.7. Cosmic eggs on the entrance of the Passmore Edwards Settlement, London, completed in 1898

8. THE OMPHALOS

To each of us, with our awareness centered in our bodies, we are at the center of our world. The place where we are at any given time is *the* place, *our* place. The observed world originates here. As each person is centered on himself or herself, so the world can be viewed as centered at a particular place. This place, like the individual, is not fixed universally for all people. Many cultures all over the Earth's round face recognize particular places as their cultural central point. In geomantic terminology, this is called by its ancient Greek name—the *omphalos*—from the story of Zeus sending two eagles to fly across the Earth's surface from side to side. Where they met was the center, and there, at Delphi, the oracle of Apollo came into being. Thus the omphalos marks the center of the Earth and the cosmos and is conceptually the navel of the world (Pennick 1979a, 23, 44–52; 1996a, 46–47; 1999a, 90, 94–99).

As a symbol the omphalos was made in the form of dome-shaped stones, sometimes garlanded with actual swags of fabric, sometimes bearing them carved into the stone, as with the omphalos at Delphi. An Etruscan omphalos at Fiesole, Italy, is shown in figure 8.1. A drawing of

Fig. 8.1. Etruscan omphalos with carved bands and hexflower, Fiesole, Italy

Fig. 8.2. Eggstone omphalos. Drawing by William Richard Lethaby. The Library of the European Tradition.

an omphalos by William Richard Lethaby is shown in figure 8.2.

A related form of geomantic central mark is the *omphalion*. Lethaby quotes Labarte's description of the omphalion in Constantinople (now Istanbul, Turkey), the center of the Christian empire of the east: "Below the dome in the pavement was a large slab of porphyry, of circular form, to which they gave the name Omphalion." Alternative names for this are *meso-naos* and *mesomphalos* (Lethaby 1891, 83–84). Directly beneath the middle of the dome of the circular Aachen Cathedral in Germany, there is an omphalion that marks the geomantic center of the Holy Roman Empire of the west. A photograph of it is shown in figure 8.3.

Fig. 8.3. The omphalion in the cathedral at Aachen, Germany

9. THE PINEAPPLE

As a classical emblem, the so-called pineapple represents the cone of the pine tree, not the tropical fruit. In older usage the word *apple* is not so specific, meaning a fruit, as in an oak apple (a gall); the French and Dutch words for potato (an "earth apple"), which are *pomme de terre* and *aardappel;* and the East Anglian dialect word *deal apple* for a pine cone. It is a symbol of fecundity and regeneration, healing and conviviality (Whittick 1971, 296), an embodiment of the sacred numbers manifested in the Fibonacci series, and related to the golden section and the pentagram, as is the geometry of the egg. The pine tree is associated with the gods Osiris and Attis, who was personified as the spirit of the tree. It is sacred to the goddess Cybele and is depicted on religious artifacts with the musical instruments of her cultus—bell, sistrum, and tambour—hanging in its branches. The wand of Dionysus is the thyrsus, a stave tipped with the pineapple. The pinecone appears in carved stone garlands and swags on Roman altars and tomb shrines, among other fruits of the Earth. As an emblem of healing, it is a minor attribute of Aesculapius, for the seed of the stone pine was an ingredient of ancient medicines. In northern Europe the pine is viewed as the tree of illumination, both on the outer level as the light-bringing flaming torch and on the inner level as understanding. In architecture it is primarily a symbol of fecundity and regeneration.

Images of pinecones surmounted Etruscan tombs, urns, and pillars (Dennis 1848, ii, 103, 157, 492). Hadrian's mausoleum in Rome was surmounted by a gilt bronze pinecone (later removed and replaced by an image of the Archangel Michael), and a Carolingian cone of bronze is preserved in the atrium of Aachen Cathedral. The pinecone is the emblem of the Swabian goddess Zisa, and numerous large stone ones survive from Roman times at Augsburg, Bavaria, Germany. One is shown in figure 9.1. The Swabian holy city of Zizarim, locus of the goddess's shrine, became the Roman city of Augusta Vindelicorum and the present-day Bavarian city of Augsburg. The *Stadtpyr* cone remains the emblem of the city, and the goddess with her cone appears as a weather vane on St. Peter-am-Perlach Church, on the site of the holy hill of the goddess. She is depicted with her cone in a classical plaque on the early seventeenth-century Hercules fountain and as the red-clad foundress of the city in a painting in the Rathaus (city hall) (Pennick 2002a, 107–9).

Fig. 9.1. Roman pineapple from Augsburg, Bavaria, Germany

10. THE TREE OF LIFE

Every tree is a living being, fixed to the Earth at a particular place for the duration of its life. Traditional spirituality venerates trees, protects and nurtures them, and makes offerings to them at appropriate times (Pennick 1979a, 18–21; Pennick 2006a, 47–52). The tree grows from the invisible underworld beneath our feet, through the Middle Earth on which we walk, and upward toward the welkin (figs. 10.1 and 10.2).

Fig. 10.1. Tree of life glyph

Fig. 10.2. Tree of life, foliated

Fig. 10.3. Tree of life on medieval tile, Waverley Abbey, Surrey

So the tree links the three worlds: below, middle, and above. Symbolically, each tree is an image of the *axis mundi,* or cosmic axis, that connects the three worlds (Pennick 1985a, 1–6). The solar halo pillar topped with a flared *V,* part of the whole sun-wheel phenomenon, is seen sometimes under certain weather conditions (Pennick 1985a, 5; Pennick 1997a, 24–26). The Saxon sacred pillar Irminsul, mentioned on page 42, partakes of some of the character of the cosmic axis and the tree of life. Images resembling Irminsul have been found on medieval tiles from ecclesiastical contexts, such as one from Waverley Abbey in Surrey (fig. 10.3), and the runelike tree is a feature of folk art all over Europe.

Another aspect of the tree of life is the jewel-bearing tree (Lethaby

Fig. 10.4. The jewel-bearing tree.
Roman bronze candelabrum.
Drawing by William Richard
Lethaby. The Library of the
European Tradition.

1891, 94–121) (fig. 10.4). Under certain conditions droplets of water adhering to the leaves, twigs, and branches of trees are illuminated by the rays of the sun, giving an appearance of sparkling jewels of many colors, twinkling as the tree moves in the breeze. Philostratus records how he saw a golden tree, with fruits represented by emeralds, which had been donated by Pygmalion, the king of Tyre, to the Temple of Hercules at Gades. Pliny notes that in the temples stood metal trees, bearing lamps, like the golden fruit of the heavens. Extant bronze candelabra of Roman times are in the form of the jewel-bearing tree, supporting lights (Lethaby 1891, 114–15), and the modern illuminated Christmas tree is its natural successor.

Two examples of metalwork from London and Loughborough, circa 1880 and 1925, respectively, depict the tree of life in different ways (fig. 10.5). That on the left, from London, has the branched form that goes back to ancient rock art, while that on the right, in the Art Deco style, is closer to the Irminsul glyph.

Some spiritual trees of life ignore the roots below the Earth, putting

Fig. 10.5. Left: Wrought-iron railing in Aesthetic style in the form of the tree of life, Fitzrovia, London; right: Art Deco wrought-iron tree of life, ca. 1930, Loughborough

Earth—that is the surface on which we live—at the bottom. But the roots of the tree are an integral part of its existence. The roots anchor the tree in the Earth, collecting the water and nutrients that sustain the tree's life. In the northern tradition, the three roots of the world tree Yggdrasil are depicted. Of the letter trees shown in figure 10.6, from three different cultures, the rune tree on the right shows its three roots. In the 1990s this rune became known as the dragon rune, though it is intended to depict the tree of life. From the Bronze Age onward, tree trunks were fashioned into coffins for the dead (Johnston 1912, 274). Allemannic examples of the *Totenbaum* (tree of the dead) in southern Germany have a serpent carved along the top of the trunk. A description

Fig. 10.6. Letter trees from three cultures: left: the Buddhist mantra *hum;* middle, Hebraic name of God; right: rune tree. Drawing by the author, 1974.

Fig. 10.7. The tree in heraldry. Left: arms on a fountain at
Schwäbisch Gmünd, Germany; right: heraldic banner, York, England.

of someone who has died is that he or she "has gone into the tree." One of
the last known interments in a tree was that of Graf von Buchaw in 1151
(Paulsen and Schach-Dörges 1972, 19–22). The heralds of both the Anglo-
French and Holy Roman Empire schools acknowledge the rootedness of
the tree, depicting it on a hill, as in the heraldic trees shown in figure 10.7:
The Schwäbisch Gmünd tree is shown growing on the triple mountain.

In the spiritual arts and crafts, the tree is shown stylistically as the
tree of life. It appears on many of the buildings of the Arts and Crafts
movement. Charles Ashbee's tree of life (fig. 10.8) depicts it bearing
fruit, a metaphor for a sustainable, humane society that cherishes kindliness above all other virtues. Its roots are acknowledged.

Fig. 10.8. Tree of life of the Guild
of Handicraft, 1889, with Charles
Ashbee's motto "To cherish
kindliness." The Library of the
European Tradition.

Fig. 10.9. Tree of life of the Institute of Geomantic Research, 1977. Poster silk-screened by the author.

The Institute of Geomantic Research, which I ran from 1975 onward, used the tree of life as its emblem (fig. 10.9) for the symbolic reasons described above.

In old Germanic culture, each family venerated a particular tree as the family tree. This was a living tree, not the term used for a genealogical record of succeeding generations, as it is used now. The tree was near the family homestead, or perhaps it predated it, for some houses were built around living trees (Davidson 1960, 4–5). The tree shown in figure 10.10, in the South Tyrol in Italy, is a classic instance of the European tradition where a tree is a spiritual center.

Fig. 10.10. Tree on a no-man's-land at a trifinium (a fork in the road) in the South Tyrol in Italy, with accompanying Christian shrine in the tradition of the European sacred landscape

Here, at a trifinium of roads is a triangular no-man's-land on which a tree grows (Pennick 1999a, 111–15; 2006b, 149; 2006a, 46). Next to it is a Christian shrine with an image of Jesus, demonstrating a continuity of spiritual tradition across religious boundaries. The village tree, known in German as a *Dorflinde* (usually a linden tree), is traditionally the central point of village life, rites, and ceremonies. In Germany and the Netherlands, it is customary to train and trim the tree to give it a number of ascending platforms of branches, resembling images of the cosmic axis (Mössinger 1938, 145–55, 388–96; Pennick 1985a, 8–10).

As the cosmic axis, the tree is a significant element in shamanism, linking the world we live on with those above and below, allowing the shaman to travel between the worlds. Trees are, of course, the natural habitat of many kinds of living birds, but drawings and artifacts from shamanic cultures also frequently depict birds as a metaphor for the soul or externalized consciousness. Christian symbolism depicts the Holy Ghost, an aspect of God, as a dove. Perhaps the stylized imagery of birds and the central tree that appears in European folk art, such as the seventeenth-century pargeted wall from Saffron Walden in Essex, shown in figure 10.11, is from a shamanic, rather than a literal, source.

Fig. 10.11. Birds and the tree of life motif, seventeenth-century
pargeting work, Saffron Walden, Essex

The use of birds and a tree is a decorative yet symbolic motif in the work of many Arts and Crafts movement artists and architects. A characteristic birds-and-trees ventilator cover design by Charles Francis Annesley Voysey from 1905 is shown in figure 10.12.

Fig. 10.12. Birds and tree of life ventilator cover by Charles Francis Annesley Voysey, 1905. The Library of the European Tradition.

The Kabbalistic tree of life is a well-known symbol of spiritual evolution and is symbolic of the cosmos in tree form, but the *catena aurea,* Homer's golden chain, shown in two versions in figure 10.13, is less a celebrated mystical tree. It is a sequence of ten sigils arranged in a descending order, a sequence that develops from chaos to quintessence.

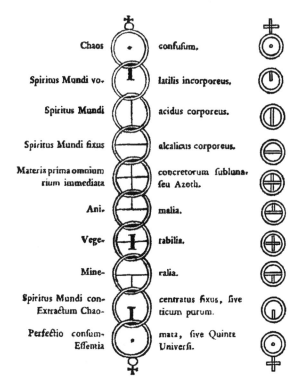

Chaos	confusum,
Spiritus Mundi vo-	latilis incorporeus,
Spiritus Mundi	acidus corporeus.
Spiritus Mundi fixus	alcalicus corporeus.
Materia prima omnium rium immediata	concretorum subluna- feu Azoth.
Ani-	malia.
Vege-	tabilia.
Mine-	ralia.
Spiritus Mundi con- Extractum Chao-	centratus fixus, five ticum purum.
Perfectio confum- Effentia	mata, five Quinte Univerfi.

Fig. 10.13. Homer's golden chain, two versions. The Library of the European Tradition.

Originating in a work of Joseph Kirchweger in 1723, the Aurea Catena Homeri is a symbolic exposition of the evolution of the cosmos, an alchemical process that the author sees as guided by God: "Before God created the system of the universe, he created by *emanation* the universal principle of light and fire with a creative instinct. . . . The first step toward materiality . . . seems to have been to generate vapor, humidity and water. This then very naturally produced chaos . . . until God moved that first principle electrically out of the chaos and it was manifested in light." Further steps in the formation of matter and the principles of existence are described, such as the spiritualization of substance through a sequence of processes, as in the transformations wrought by the alchemists (McLean 1979, 21–22; Colquhoun 1979, 15–17). First, at the top is chaos. Below this comes the volatile spirit of the Earth; next, Earthy acid spirit; then fixed earthy spirit. The fifth sigil, the quartered square (sun wheel, Celtic cross) denotes the primary substance of all bodies. Beneath this come the animal, vegetable, and mineral; next is the pure, concentrated fixed earthy tincture, the *extractum chaoticum,* and finally, the perfect concentrated universal quintessence. The catena aurea uses sigils that are immediately recognizable as part of the European tradition, yet with other meanings.

11. THE FLEUR-DE-LYS

This glyph is closely connected with French royalty, appearing as a heraldic sign on the coats of arms of France and on the French battle flag, the Oriflamme (fig. 11.1). The pattern is older than France or heraldry, for a version of it appeared on military belt buckles manufactured for the Roman Army, an example of which is shown in figure 11.2.

Fig. 11.1. The fleur-de-lys

Fig. 11.2. Roman Army belt-buckle motif, fourth century, with early fleur-de-lys motifs. Drawing by the author.

Of course there are many variations, but some approach the form later designated as the fleur-de-lys. Later it appeared in Viking-era art, where it was called the union knot. Some Anglo-Saxon brooches have floriated appendages that approach the fleur-de-lys form, such as the sixth-century one with a swastika from Sleaford, Lincolnshire, shown in figure 11.3.

Fig. 11.3. Anglo-Saxon brooch from Sleaford, Lincolnshire. The Library of the European Tradition.

A model bronze tombstone found in the Thames at Hammersmith, dating from the tenth century and in the Ringerike style, is topped by a union knot that is indistinguishable from the fleur-de-lys. This form of pagan tombstone was prevalent in Frisia until the early twentieth century, such as those at Wanneperveen, the Netherlands (Von Zaborsky 1936, 185–95; Wirth 1931–1936, vol. 7, 720, pls. 372, 372A). Because it was used by the kings of France, it was taken into English royal heraldry from the times when English kings claimed the throne of France. Along with the swastika, in the early twentieth century, the fleur-de-lys was adopted by Lord Robert Baden-Powell as an emblem of the Boy Scout movement. The Scout fleur-de-lys has five-pointed stars in the two horizontal leaves. The fleur-de-lys is a motif in eastern English pargeting, generally stamped, appearing both as single glyphs among different motifs and as an overall regular pattern, as in the photo from Cambridge in figure 11.4.

Fig. 11.4. Fleur-de-lys-stamped pargeting on a shop in Cambridge

12. THE ROSE

Members of the genus *Rosaceae,* the rose family of plants, have fivefold geometry in their flowers and fruits. This links them to sacred geometry, which expresses the fivefold as the pentagram and the related golden section, embodied within its proportions (Pennick 1980c, 25–28; 2005b, 64–65). This unique, infinitely reproducible proportion gives the fivefold structure of the rose a special place in sacred geometry, seen as the emanation of the principle of growth, or the mind of God in tangible form (fig. 12.1).

Fig. 12.1. The rose

Fig. 12.2. The rose as emblem of England, with the shield with the Cross of St. George. Wood engraving by I. de B. Lockyer, early twentieth century. The Library of the European Tradition.

The pentagram is the basic geometric form embodied in the rose. The rose has a significant place in alchemy, heraldry, and the Rosicrucian mysteries (fig. 12.2). In 1485 it was adopted by King Henry VII as the emblem of the Tudor dynasty. The College of Heralds amalgamated the red rose of Lancaster with the white rose of York to create a double rose as the glyph of the Tudors. The single red rose shown in this engraving, circa 1920, stands symbolically for England today. The white rose of York flies proudly on Yorkshire flags, and the black-and-white Yorkshire battle flag carried on a spear under fire onto a Normandy beach on D-Day in 1944 during World War II is shown in figure 12.3.

Fig. 12.3. The battle flag of Yorkshire, black with white rose and small anchor, carried under enemy fire onto the Normandy beaches on D-Day, June 1944

In 1598 in his *Amphitheatrum Sapientiæ Æternæ,* Heinrich Khunrath published nine "singular pantacles" emblematic of the alchemical process. The fifth of these is the rose of light, in the middle of which is a human with arms in the form of a cross. Élephas Lévi, in his *Histoire de la Magie,* commented on the symbolism of the rose: "The rose, in fact, is a pantacle; its form is circular, the leaves of the corolla are heart-shaped . . . the reunion of the rose and the cross, such was the problem proposed by supreme initiation, and, in effect, occult philosophy, being the universal synthesis, should take into account all the phenomena of being" (Lévi, quoted in Waite 1887, 23). "From the time of the Guelphs and the Ghibellines a common device in heraldry is the Rose-Emblem," noted Arthur Edward Waite. "It figures on our English coins; it is used as a royal badge in the Civil War between the houses of York and Lancaster; it is associated above all with the great mediæval cultus of the Mother of God, being our Lady's flower *par excellence,* as the lily is characteristic of St. Joseph" (Waite 1887, 17) (fig. 12.4).

Fig. 12.4. Heraldic rose and sigil on printer's mark of Peter Schoiffher of Mentz, early sixteenth century, where the top two roses replaced the six-pointed stars in his predecessors' marks, there having been but a single rose in them. The mark was granted to the family by the emperor of the Holy Roman Empire, Maximilian. The Library of the European Tradition.

Symbolically, the rose is primarily an emblem of Our Lady. Our Lady, in Christian terms, the mother of Jesus, is symbolized by the infinitely expansive fivefold geometry, the glyph of limitless generation, according to which the physical rose flowers (fig. 12.5).

Fig. 12.5. Rosicrucian ritual jewel in the form of a Latin cross, nineteenth century. The Library of the European Tradition.

The rose as a ceiling emblem signifies silence. The expression *sub rosa* (beneath the rose) means that anything said in a room with such an emblem is not to be repeated anywhere else. A pargeted ceiling rose in a sixteenth-century house in Ludlow, Shropshire, is illustrated in figure 12.6. Waite notes an explanatory myth that *sub rosa* "originated in the ancient dedication of the flower to Aphrodite, and its reconsecration by Cupid to Harpocrates, the tutelary deity of silence, to induce him to conceal the amours of the goddess of love" (Waite 1887, 18).

Fig. 12.6. Ceiling rose, sixteenth century, in private house, Ludlow, Shropshire

The rose tree is a thorn tree, and it is the thorn of the rose that appears in the futhark as the rune *thorn*. Naturally, in rune magic it is a rune of protection, warding off harm and preventing intrusion through its power of enclosure. It is this meaning that we find in *sub rosa*. As the phonetic glyph for "th," it is the only rune that continues in everyday public use in England, in the definitive article *Ye*, as, for instance, in the celebrated London pub Ye Olde Cheshire Cheese. The first character is

Fig. 12.7. The thorn rune

Fig. 12.8. Thorns of the wild rose

Fig. 12.9. Rose, thistle, and shamrock, emblems of England, Scotland, and Ireland. Pargeting, Dunmow, Essex.

Fig. 12.10. Rose mosaic designed by the author, Germany, 1992

not a phonetic *Y*, however much people mispronounce it, but the *thorn* rune (figs. 12.7 and 12.8).

Pargeted roses on the exterior of a building, such as those on a shop in Dunmow, Essex, seen in figure 12.9, do not have the connotation of silence. Here the rose clearly stands for England, as the accompanying glyphs are the Scots thistle and the Irish shamrock. A rose mosaic that I designed and constructed in Germany in 1992 with full rites and ceremonies is shown in figure 12.10.

The Rosicrucian movement or fraternity, or people claiming continuity with it, went public in France in the late nineteenth century as part of a general spiritual reawakening that included symbolist art and literature. Their events were artistic as well as mystical in character and had a lasting influence. During the early nineteenth century, canal artists in England and Wales adopted the rose as a main emblem in their decoration of narrowboats (Lewery 1996, 30). The expression "roses and castles" is a name given to this form of people's art (Robert J. Wilson 1976, 4–11; Lewery 1996, 38–49). A narrowboat used as a houseboat on the river at Cambridge, *Tumbling Water,* is illustrated in figure 12.11.

Fig. 12.11. Traditional English canal art in the form of roses and ornamental lettering on a narrowboat moored at Cambridge, 2005

In the late nineteenth century, perhaps through Rosicrucian influence, the mystic rose was adopted as an emblem by designers, architects, and stained-glass artists. Medieval masters of Gothic architecture had created stunning circular geometric windows in cathedrals, which the master glaziers filled with jewels of light. These are known as rose windows, though the rose itself rarely appears overtly in them (Cowen 1979). But the nineteenth- and twentieth-century glass designers used the rose itself emblematically. The work of Charles Rennie Mackintosh and Margaret MacDonald Mackintosh is replete with stylized roses. A 1903 leaded-glass window by Alexander Gascoygne is illustrated in figure 12.12.

Fig. 12.12. Leaded-glass window with roses, designed by Alexander Gascoygne, 1903. The Library of the European Tradition.

13. THE HEART

Although it is the organ that physically pumps blood around the body, the heart is primarily a symbol of affection, love, and devotion (fig. 13.1). The Stoic philosophy sees the heart as the seat of the human soul, and the soul reciprocally as the exhalation of the blood. Astrologically, the heart corresponds with the sun, ruled by the astrological sign Leo. In contemporary imagery the glyph is understood as the sign of love and the lucky heart (Von Zaborsky 1936, 120–28; Peesch 1983, 108–16).

Fig. 13.1. The heart

This is not a new departure. The *offrande du cœur*, the lover's heart as a gift to his beloved, was a popular image in the works of the medieval troubadours. Medieval French books of love songs were bound with covers tooled with the heart glyph. The goddess of love, Venus, was depicted with a flaming heart in emblematical engravings in the Renaissance period (e.g., those by Jörg Bentz, Nuremberg, Germany, ca. 1529). One of the symbolic carvings in the *pleasaunce* (rose-garden or pleasure garden) at Edzell Castle, near Brechin, Scotland, made in 1604, is Venus with a flaming heart, seemingly derived from Bentz (Simpson 1933, 17–24).

The Sacred Heart of Jesus was added to the repertoire of heart motifs in 1675 by Marguerite Marie Alacoque (1647–1690), a Roman Catholic nun in the convent of Parray-le-Monial, later canonized by the pope as St. Marguerite Marie. Figure 13.2 shows the image made by St. Marguerite Marie herself in 1685, recording what she had beheld in a vision. At the center is the heart. From it emanate rays and a cross. Inside the heart, stoked by the flames and guarded by spikes, is the virtue of charity. The heart is itself surrounded by a garland or crown of thorns (Pennick 2002c, 30–31, 33).

This Catholic image was preceded by alchemical emblems such as that of the French alchemist Nicolas Flamel, which was a heart from

Fig. 13.2. *The Sacred Heart*. Drawing by St. Marguerite Marie, originator of the cult of St. Marguerite Marie. The Library of the European Tradition.

which grows a plant, surrounded by a garland of thorns. Two alchemical glyphs in David L'Agneau's *Harmonie Mystique,* published in Paris in 1636, show a five-wounded heart surrounded by thorns. Thus an image of Catholic piety was taken from the hermetic tradition. The human heart may be depicted with flames issuing forth from it. Prospero Lorenzo Lambertini (Pope Benedict XIV), who was pontiff between 1740 and 1758, promoted the doctrine of bodily fire in his tract *De Beatificatione et Canonizatione:* "From a man's whole person fire may occasionally radiate naturally, not, however like a flame that streams upward, but rather in the form of sparks which are given off all round." Illustrated in figure 13.3 is

Fig. 13.3. Evil in the human heart, emblematic engraving from a German religious tract of 1846. The Library of the European Tradition.

a nineteenth-century print from a hellfire German religious tract of 1846, warning that the human heart has two possibilities. It can become, the author asserts, either the temple of God or the workshop of Satan. Here the heart is shown as the latter, ruled by the devil and the seven deadly sins, emblematized as animals.

The heart pierced by the arrow of Cupid is a motif well known from traditional British tattoos. The emblem of the Guild of Nail-Makers in Germany is a heart pierced by three nails, a Christian emblem of the wounds of Jesus. English folk art sometimes uses the heart shape for pincushions, with the pins ornamentally arranged (Lewery 1991, 104). A heart-shaped piece of cloth stuck with pins has been found among the contents of a witch bottle from Ipswich (Bunn 1982, 4). Mummified hearts of cattle and pigs stuck with thorns or pins have been found as house deposits (objects deliberately placed in the foundations, walls, or chimneys of houses) in Cambridgeshire, Dorset, London, and Somerset (Elworthy 1895, 53–54; Rushen 1984, 35; Brian Hoggard, personal communication). In some cases these were charms used in the magical cure of sick animals (March 1899, 483; Dacombe 1935, 109–10). Elworthy records a custom that when a pig died from the evil eye, its heart was stuck with pins and white thorns, and it was put up the chimney "in the belief that as the heart dried and withered so would that of the malignant person who had 'ill wisht' the pig" (Elworthy 1895, 53).

The heart signifies one of the four suits of playing cards that bear the familiar glyphs (fig. 13.4). These four suits originated in the French decks of the seventeenth century with the suits *coeurs, piques, carreaux,* and *trèfles* (hearts, spades, diamonds, and clubs) (Hamilton 1988, 16–17).

Fig. 13.4. "Poker" card suits, of French origin

Fig. 13.5. Central European card suits

Fig. 13.6. Traditional biscuit-making stamp in the form of an ornament heart, Stuttgart, Baden-Württemberg, Germany

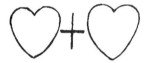

Fig. 13.7. Heart and crissross pattern, from Elworthy. The Library of the European Tradition.

Fig. 13.8. Somerset vegetable-planting mark

Hearts, acorns, bells, and leaves are the suits in Central European decks (fig. 13.5), while the Spanish playing card deck has the tarot suits: cups, swords, coins, and batons (clubs). As a shape the heart glyph is close to a leaf. I have mentioned the case of the coat of arms of the kings of Frisia in the "New Names, New Meanings" section of this book (page 25), where water-lily leaves became hearts (Commission of the Fryske Akademy 1956, 62).

The heart is a common motif in European and American folk art (Lipman and Meulendyke 1951; Peesch 1983, 108–16). A wooden biscuit-making stamp from Baden-Württemberg, Germany, shown in figure 13.6, has motifs within a heart shape, carded so they appear in relief on the finished confection.

Two hearts and a crisscross, a glyph of two hearts with a cross between them, shown in figure 13.7, is recorded by Frederick Thomas Elworthy as a charm used in brewing. It was drawn on the surface of the mash before it was covered up to ferment, to ward off the pixies, as Elworthy's Somerset "old man" said. The same glyph and a variant with one heart (fig. 13.8) are used to mark seedbeds where special seeds are sown (Elworthy 1895, 287).

In the early twentieth century, the noted architect Charles Francis Annesley Voysey used the heart motif as a letter plate on his houses' front doors to signify that profound spiritual love is the source of creativity.

This is the meaning of the heart-shaped sound holes common in mountain dulcimers of the Appalachians, illustrated in figure 13.9.

Fig. 13.9. Heart-shaped and heart-derived-shaped sound holes on two mountain dulcimers: left, made by Stony Ridge, U.S.A., right, by Paul Hathway, London

When four hearts are arranged point to point, then the glyph of the four-leaf clover appears. Figure 13.10 shows the clover as a glyph in pargeting work on the walls of the old Blue Boar Inn in Cambridge.

Fig. 13.10. Heart-leaf patterns in pargeting work on the old Blue Boar Inn, Cambridge

14. HUMAN AND ELDRITCH HEADS

The ancient Celts practiced the cult of the head, where the severed heads of slain enemies were preserved as trophies. Preserved in the Celto-Ligurian shrine at Roqueperteuse in the south of France were human skulls embedded within niches hewn in the megaliths. The miraculous head of Bran the Blessed, which continued to give oracles after it was severed, appears in the ancient Welsh story *Branwen, Daughter of Llyr*. After being carried around Wales, the head was finally brought to London and buried in the White Mount, where the Tower of London now stands, after which it became the magical protector of Britain against its enemies.

Fig. 14.1. Head of St. Edmund with military trophies, eighteenth-century sculpted panel, Bury St. Edmunds, Suffolk

Centuries later, the head of the East Anglian king and saint, Edmund, was recovered by his followers from his execution place and enshrined in the holy city of Bury St. Edmunds. An eighteenth-century icon of St. Edmund, surrounded by trophies, is shown in figure 14.1.

Heads that appear on buildings sometimes serve the function that Bran's did. The head over the fortified gateway of the medieval fortified town Rothenburg shown in figure 14.2 is an example. Heads that appear on buildings also recall real human heads that once served to display power and retribution and warn others not to take the risk. Severed heads of executed noblemen and rebels were impaled on iron spikes and displayed at the gates of London and York. London has a long tradition of head display. After Oliver Cromwell's corpse was exhumed and desecrated, his head loomed on a pike end over Westminster Hall for decades as a warning to others. And until the middle of the eighteenth century, heads of executed Jacobites were spiked on Temple Bar.

Some have asserted that each being carved on a building in a traditional way is ensouled with its peculiar spirit. The magical technique of gargoyle evocation, ascribed to the apocryphal Canon Fadge, claims to deal with the powers of these eldritch figures, none of which have

Fig. 14.2. Mask over fortified gatehouse of Rothenburg, Germany

any harmful nature, we are told, despite their grotesque gargoyled appearance (Fadge 1979; Symon 1979, 19–21). The bizarre being from Wisbech, Cambridgeshire, shown in figure 14.3 is typical.

Fig. 14.3. Medieval demonic jester figure or gargoyle, Wisbech, Cambridgeshire

Allied to these figures are the foliate heads and heads looking out through foliage that everyone calls the green man, even the female images of St. Frideswide hiding in the forest whose remains are preserved in Oxford Cathedral. A head at the Abbey of Maulbronn in Germany is shown in figure 14.4, looking out at us through the leaves of the Mirkwood.

Fig. 14.4. Medieval foliate head, monastic cloister, Maulbronn, Germany

During the seventeenth century, the classical principles of geomancy and architecture were used in the design of new churches for London after the Great Fire and for the country estates of the nobility. In the early eighteenth century, architectural urns with apotropaic masks facing the four cardinal directions were designed by Sir Christopher Wren,

Fig. 14.5. Four-faced urn designed by Sir John Vanbrugh and formerly on the destroyed Temple of Sleep at Stowe, Buckinghamshire

Nicholas Hawksmoor, and Sir John Vanbrugh for church towers and the finials of temples and monuments. One of Vanbrugh's surviving artifacts is the four-faced urn of 1719 from the destroyed Temple of Sleep at Stowe, Buckinghamshire, shown in figure 14.5 (Pennick 2005b, 107).

In traditional ritual and spiritual performance, participants frequently wear masks that serve to disguise the wearer's individuality, transforming him or her into an impersonal type. Ancient Greek theater had masked performers, and such a mask is shown in figure 14.6. The stark reality of the mask expresses an archetypal energy, engendering rapture and terror in anyone who beholds it.

Fig. 14.6. Ancient Greek theatrical mask

In ancient times funeral masks were set over the faces of the departed, and the masked dead were thus personated at times when the ancestral spirits were ritually honored. Sometimes, the mask denoted kinghood, as in the magnificent metal mask found in the Anglian royal burial at Sutton Hoo. For no ordinary person may behold the true face of the gods or of the otherworldly dead: there must be an outer covering for the unseeable spirit. And in times when the gods were officially denied, their images were carved in churches and stamped on earthenware vessels that sometimes those who knew took and used for magical purposes.

There is a spiritual power in masks, for each time a mask is donned, the wearer represents the masked archetype, whether it signifies the ancestor or the dead, a divinity or power, or a being of the eldritch world. The masked person is a nameless being enacting a ritual role, an incarnation of the spirit depicted by the mask. The boundary line between human beings, lifeless effigies, ensouled images of deities, and uncanny beings is always fluid and uncertain. The masked one stands in the liminal space at the meeting point of the present and the past, the personal and the collective, the living and the dead, this world and the otherworld. The mask enacts a dialogue between two sides of existence: the container and the contained, the exterior and the interior, the seen and the unseen. For the duration of the masquerade, the masker personates the *mask's* character. The mask wearer's identity is subordinated to the power signified by the mask. Whatever the personation signifies, the performance itself takes place in the here and now and is operative by its present effects. Masks are representations of eternal, archetypal things, yet present in the here and now, keeping up the day. In springtime in the German *Schwarzwald,* the keepers perform the rite of Awakening the Masks when they take them out from their winter hiding places in preparation for their annual outing. Now their moment has come round again when they will awaken and again personate their characters publicly. These traditional masks, carved from particular woods by hereditary masters of the art, are ensouled in their own right, and those that wear them are fully aware of it. Figures 14.7 and 14.8 show two contemporary masks worn at carnival events.

Fig. 14.7. Masked fellow appearing at the Fastnacht (Shrovetide carnival) at Rottenburg, Germany

Fig. 14.8. The author wearing a long-snouted mask at the Venice carnival, made from papier-mâché covered with gold leaf

15. THE SWASTIKA

The swastika, *svastika,* or *sauvastika,* otherwise known as the fylfot, *fyrfos, gammadion,* four-footed cross, or tetraskelion, and in heraldry as the cross potent rebated, is an often misunderstood glyph because of its use by the German National Socialists between 1919 and 1945 (figs. 15.1 and 15.2).

Fig. 15.1. The swastika, short-armed form

Fig. 15.2. Heraldic cross potent rebated from a nineteenth-century work on heraldry. The Library of the European Tradition.

However, as I noted in the "New Names, New Meanings" section in Part I of this book (page 25), the swastika is by no means to be defined solely by one of its many historical uses any more than any other glyph is. Historical opinions and uses are all part of a glyph's history but do not define it once and for all as having a certain fixed meaning.

For centuries Catholic priests officiated at the Mass wearing vestments covered with swastikas, as shown by a fragment of medieval memorial brass (fig. 15.3) from Great Leigh, Essex (Piggot 1870, 9). But now no Christian priest wears the glyph. Similarly, it appeared on the memorial shields of English knights, including Sir John Daubernon (1277) and Sir Thomas de Hop (ca. 1370).

Fig. 15.3. Fragment of medieval memorial brass from Great Leigh, Essex, showing a clergyman in his vestment with swastikas. The Library of the European Tradition.

From the nineteenth century onward, the swastika became of great interest to researchers into esoteric matters. Opinions on the meaning of the glyph are many. There are numerous books and articles written by occult, esoteric, political, and religious authors about the swastika, and the subject is by no means exhausted (e.g., Pennick 1979b; Taylor 2006).

In northern Europe the swastika has been long associated with the god of thunder. In 1884 Robert Philips Greg wrote of it in *On the Meaning and Origin of the Fylfot and Swastika*. Two years later

H. Colley March of the Lancashire and Cheshire Antiquarian Society wrote about it in his paper "The Fylfot and the Futhorc Tyr"; and in 1888 Llewellyn Jewitt commented:

In northern mythology the Fylfot is known as the Hammer of Thorr, the Scandinavian god, or Thunderer, and is called "Thorr's Hammer" or the "Thunderbolt." The emblem of this god, Thorr or the Thunderer, was . . . a thunderbolt or a hammer of gold, which hammer was frequently represented by a Fylfot. (Jewitt 1984)

In 1895 Frederick Thomas Elworthy in *The Evil Eye* gave his opinion of the swastika's meaning: "There are other kinds of cross among the variety used in heraldry or ornament, which certainly have a mystery about them, and some of which are amulets. . . . Foremost among these is the *svastika* of the Hindus, the fylfot-cross or gammadion, called also by some the 'catch L.' Among the Hindus this was the mark of Vishnu, the beneficent preserver of life. . . . This form of cross was early adopted among Christian symbols, for it is found in the Roman catacombs of the fourth century. . . . From its appearance on coins and from its being a sun sign we may accept the conclusion that the *fylfot* was an amulet against the evil eye" (Elworthy 1895, 289–90). Guido List in 1910 classified the fyrfos as his second *Ur-Glyphe* (primal glyph). He saw it as a fire sign, one of the most holy signs of Armanendom. List gives other names of the sign: *Hakenkreuz* (hook cross), *Thuask,* and *Svastika* (List 1910, vol. 1, 43–44). Edred Thorsson categorizes the swastika among the "quadraplectic signs" that signify the sky, the sun, and lightning and notes that the swastika is called *sólarhvél* (sun wheel) and *Thórshamárr* in Old Norse (Thorsson 1993, 14). Thórshamarr also appears in a different form that still has some resemblance to the swastika, used as a magical glyph (fig. 15.4) (Thorsson 1993, 15; Taylor 2006, cover illustration, 79–80).

Fig. 15.4. The *Thórshamarr* glyph

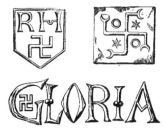

Fig. 15.5. Medieval English bell-foundry marks with swastikas. The Library of the European Tradition.

The swastika was used as a house mark of bell founders in England, mainly in the shires of Derby, Lincoln, Nottingham, Stafford, and York. The foundry owned by the Heathcote family in Chesterfield used the sign for at least four generations in the sixteenth century (Taylor 2006, 77–80, 163). There are medieval inscriptions on bells that invoke warding power against storms (fig. 15.5). "As the ringing of the church bells in times of tempest was superstitiously believed to drive away thunder, probably the old Thunderer superstition that had not died out of the popular mind might have had something to do with the putting there on the sign of Thorr, who was believed to have power over storms and tempests, and of himself throwing the thunderbolts" (Jewitt 1984). Smiths have used the pattern in protective ironwork of window grilles and gateways, perhaps to serve the same function against the flash (figs. 15.6 and 15.7).

Fig. 15.6. Fylfot patterns in wrought-iron window grille, sixteenth century, Colmar, Alsace, France

Fig. 15.7. Swastika ironwork on a nineteenth-century park gate
at Richmond, Surrey

Guido List published a diagram of the deconstruction of the sun wheel into four symbolic quarters, which could be reconstituted as the fyrfos, which he described as the spiral of life, signifying fate or destiny (Balzli 1917, 7). Ludwig Wilser's slim volume *Das Hakenkreuz nach Ursprung, Vorkommen, und Bedeutung* of 1918 also makes the solar connection, illustrating a sun wheel and swastika from the catacombs of Rome (Wilser 1918, 5). In his *The Book of Signs,* Rudolf Koch said the swastika was derived from the sun wheel and used by early Christians as a disguised cross in the days when the religion was persecuted: hence the name *crux dissimulata* (Koch 1930, 18). Because Hitler had used the swastika as the emblem of the National Socialists, many German-language writers of that era were keen to write popular books about its origin and meaning, most of them very speculative in their analysis. In 1936 Oskar Von Zaborsky, who saw the swastika as a sun wheel, linked it with the *Wenderad,* the sign called the *skirl* by Sir Flinders Petrie (Petrie 1930, LI, LII; Von Zaborsky 1936, 30–33). By far the most unexpected of these commentators was the last German emperor, Kaiser Wilhelm II (Wilhelm Hohenzollern), who, after his abdication, lived in exile in the Netherlands until his death in 1941. Hohenzollern's book about the swastika was titled *Die chinesische Monade: Ihre Geschichte und ihre Deutung* and was published in Leipzig in 1934.

In his book *The Occult Causes of the Present War,* in which he portrayed both German culture in general and Nazism in particular as satanically inspired, Lewis Spence stated that the swastika "is not only a most ancient pagan device, but is well known as a satanist symbol—'the broken cross'—typifying, as it does, the Christian cross defaced . . . it is unquestionably to be found in numerous *grimoires* and magical books of the more demonic kind" (Spence 1941, 108). The United Kingdom was at that time engaged in a war of survival against a ruthless enemy, and the propaganda of war is not known for its accuracy or temperate language, being another weapon in the arsenal. The myth that the swastika was reversed by Adolf Hitler to make it an evil sign also appears to have originated in World War II propaganda, perhaps attributable to H. G. Wells. Historically, the swastika has appeared in both forms equally, but with the form used by Hitler seen as taking precedence. In 1930 Sir Flinders Petrie categorized the swastika in the direction the Nazis used it as the *forward* form, and the other way round as *backward* (Petrie 1930, LXIX–LXX). Taylor classifies Petrie's forward swastika as recto, and the backward one as verso (Taylor 2006, 15–16) (fig. 15.8). The pre-Nazi book by Wilser (1918), whose cover is shown in figure 15.9, used the forward form, which appeared more frequently than the backward one at that period.

In the nineteenth century, before Madame Helen P. Blavatsky popularized it, the swastika had been used for around 1,700 years as a Christian sign, as mentioned by Koch in 1930.

Fig. 15.8. Equal-armed swastikas, recto (left) and verso (right)

Fig. 15.9. Book cover of Ludwig Wilser's pre-Nazi *Das Hakenkreuz nach Ursprung, Vorkommen, und Bedeutung* (1918)

The Round Church in Cambridge was completely rebuilt in 1841, and a leaded-glass window dating from that time still has its Christian swastikas. It was designed by the heraldic artist Thomas Willement (Taylor 2006, 58–59). Three swastikas were in the backward form and one in the foreward. When the window was damaged in the 1980s, the forward one was replaced by a backward one, probably because of the Nazi use of the foreward form. Thus the 3 + 1 symbolism common in Christian quaternaries was no longer followed. The photograph in figure 15.10 was taken in 1959 by Rupert Pennick when the window was in its original condition.

Fig. 15.10. Swastikas in a stained-glass window in the Holy Sepulchre (Round) Church, Cambridge, 1959. Photograph by Rupert Pennick. The Library of the European Tradition.

The swastika is a Finnish national sign, and aircraft of the Finnish Air Force long carried the emblem. Finland's state honor, the Suomen Valkoisen Ruusun ritarikunta (Order of the White Rose) was instituted in 1919 by Baron Carl Gustav Mannerheim. When designed in 1919, the collar of the order worn by a commander grand cross was composed of white roses alternating with equal-armed swastikas. The swastikas were replaced in 1963 by eightfold sigils representing spruce branches (Hieronymussen and Strüwing 1967, 49, 129–31). In 1922, long before

Fig. 15.11. *The Circle of the Aeons.* Gustav Wolf, 1922.

the canner's logo was devised, Gustav Wolf's symbolic drawing *Der Kreis der Aeonen* (*The Circle of the Aeons*) (fig. 15.11) used the swastika as an emblem of movement.

In 1969 I was a participant in an alternative press syndicate, the Cambridge Native Press. This group of autonomous magazines circled around the "underground newspaper" *Cambridge Voice,* which I was involved with from its beginning in the previous year. Among the publications issued under the Cambridge Native Press aegis was the poetry and literary magazine *Swastika,* for which I did artwork. The first issue appeared in March 1969. In the first issue, the editor, Christopher Crutchley, wrote:

> Welcome to the first edition of *Swastika,* the new Cambridge poetry and literary magazine. First let it be said that this mag is *not* Nazi propaganda as the title might suggest to those who can only remember the last war. Cast your mind back further than that, and some of you will already know that the swastika has been used as a religious symbol connected with fertility for 10,000 years. This symbol must be re-instated in society—but with its original meaning.

We decided at the time to use the commonly understood Sanskrit name, swastika, rather than fylfot, fyrfos, gammadion, and so on, and I have continued this in my subsequent writings on the subject. (Pennick 1975; 1979b; 1989b, 209; 1999b, 8, 43, 81). The back cover of *Swastika* number 2, April 1969, is reproduced in figure 15.12.

Fig. 15.12. Magazine back cover, *Swastika* number 2, April 1969. Artwork by the author. The Library of the European Tradition.

The movement in Cambridge at that time to reinstate the swastika was, of course, controversial. At an open-air art exhibition in Christ's Pieces Park that summer, among other of my paintings, I exhibited one of a swastika in a pop art style. The reaction was that "some stared incredulous. Others complained and the word 'affront' was used" (Pennick 1979b, 1). It gave me an opportunity to discuss the many meanings of the sign. Later, in January 1972, the same painting appeared at an exhibition of work of the Birkenhead Dada group at the Everyman Theatre in Liverpool, which was closed down as scandalous by the theater management after only three hours.

The curved glyph made from a continuous line and containing nine dots is sometimes called a swastika. One of the apparently oldest instances of the glyph, the pattern on a rock at Ilkley, Yorkshire, was illustrated by J. Romilly Allen in his 1904 book *Celtic Art in Pagan and Christian Times* (fig. 15.13). It is presumed to be from the Bronze Age, on account of similar carvings of that era in Sweden, though it has been found as graffiti in medieval churches. Romilly Allen called it a "Winding Band (curved Swastika)" and connected it with Mycenaean and Scandinavian patterns composed of winding bands with small bosses or dots (Romilly Allen 1904, 57–58). Figure 15.13 shows how

Fig. 15.13. The Ilkley swastika. Drawing by J. Romilly Allen, 1904. The Library of the European Tradition.

this pattern actually has ten depressions or dots and a second line that is integral with it.

So should this image be ranked with curving glyphs that are made from a single line with nine dots? This is the problem of selectivity, of seeing what we want to see and then describing it in terms of what we already know. The standard pattern to which Romilly Allen was referring is a curving pattern drawn around nine dots arranged in a cross with one in the middle. In the early 1980s, I determined the relationship between this curvilinear glyph, the shield knot, and the classical (Cretan) labyrinth pattern, via a cross composed of nine dots that is the common starting point of all (Pennick 1984b, 4). I used this glyph when I painted the signboard of Runestaff Crafts (fig. 15.14) with the dots colored according to directions in the ancient British color system.

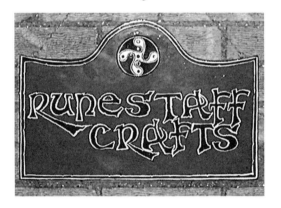

Fig. 15.14. Runestaff Crafts signboard, painted by the author, June 3, 1984

Known as the Celtic rose or Camunian rose in the context of the rock carvings at Val Camonica in Italy, this sign has also been called an ogee swastika. Anyone who has seen the palimpsest of carvings and scribings in the Camunian Valley will know how hard it is to distinguish one glyph from another, and the Celtic rose illustrated by Emmanuel Anati shows more than nine dots and an animal-life shape drawn seemingly as part of the pattern (Anati 1976, 136). As the glyph in its simplest form is not exclusive to Val Camonica anyway, this is another instance of names that express the spectacle of attachment to a particular place when they are found in many other, different contexts. And it is not called a Celtic rose in Britain, where supposedly Celtic ones actually exist. There it tends to be called a

Fig. 15.15. Medieval graffito, Sutton, Bedfordshire. The Library of the European Tradition.

fylfot to distinguish it from rectilinear swastikas. It appears as part of a medieval graffito in the church at Sutton in Bedfordshire, where it is on a figure that may be meant to show or record a performance of some kind (fig. 15.15).

A similar glyph, where there are no dots but bulbously curved ends of crossing lines, is claimed as a Basque sign and often called the Basque cross, *signe oviphile,* or *lauburu* (Taylor 2006, 21, 32, 101, 147). However, like most signs ascribed a particular identity, this glyph is not exclusively from the Basque country. Figure 15.16 shows the entrance of a barn in Hofgeismar in Westphalia, Germany, dated 1818, carved and painted with this glyph, a six-pointed star, and a budlike pattern.

Fig. 15.16. Barn at Hofgeismar, Germany, with sigils including the fylfot and dated July 17, 1818

Oskar Von Zaborsky illustrates an 1848 tombstone in Gohfeld, Kreis Herford, Germany, with this glyph inside an eighteenfold sunburst (Von Zaborsky 1936, 28, fig. 48). In Germany one of its names is *Bauernhakenkreuz* (the farmer's hook cross).

16. THE SKIRL, YIN AND YANG

Related to the previous swastika glyph is the skirl, alternatively the whorl (fig. 16.1). Some sixth-century memorial stones on the Baltic island of Gotland have painted representations of this skirl as the major feature, and slightly later Irish manuscripts incorporate Celtic skirls in their illuminations (fig. 16.2).

Fig. 16.1.
The skirl pattern

Fig. 16.2.
Skirl, Ireland, vignette
from *The Book of Durrow*

Petrie notes that the skirl seems to be intended to denote circular motion, as in a Hittite drawing of a chariot wheel he illustrates and in the name *Wenderad* that is used by Von Zaborsky (Petrie 1930, 7; LI, P T9; Von Zaborsky 1936, 30–33). Élephas Lévi called it the "whirlwind of fire," one of the stages in the process of creation. The skirl made of three curving lines has been connected with the swastika by some writers and by others to the *valknut,* a glyph composed of three interlocking equilateral triangles, generally associated with Scandinavia (Von Zaborsky 1936, 30–33; Thorsson 1993, 12). In folk art skirls are often related to spirals, as visible in the ancient carved panel in the church at Skenfrith, Herefordshire, shown in figure 16.3.

Fig. 16.3. Spiral panel, Skenfrith, Herefordshire, eighteenth century

    Fig. 16.4. Yin and yang glyph

The Chinese glyph yin and yang (fig. 16.4), signifying the interdependence of opposites, has long been known in Europe. This glyph may have been transmitted at an early date or developed independently in the western Roman Empire, as it is shown as one of the legionary shield glyphs in *Notitia Dignitatum,* a copy of a fifth-century manuscript by Guido Panciroli, published at Lyon in 1606. The glyph appears as the emblem of the legion called Mauri Officinaci (Panciroli 1606, 127). The yin and yang glyph was fully assimilated in the West during the nineteenth century, appearing in syncretic magical diagrams, mainly in France. During the 1950s, the postwar interest in Buddhism, especially by the beatniks, led to yin and yang appearing in ephemeral publications and even in the logo of the antiapartheid movement. The short-lived mural illustrated in figure 16.5 was on the end wall of a shop rented by the Beatles in 1968. The psychedelic mural by Marijke Koger has many cosmic and psychic glyphs, including, on the figure's chest, a yin and yang in complementary red and blue. It was made without planning permission and was vengefully destroyed by the authorities within weeks of being painted.

Fig. 16.5. Mural by Marijke Koger on the Beatles' shop, London, 1968. Destroyed.

17. THE POTHOOK

The hake, hanger, or pothook is an implement used to suspend pots and kettles over the kitchen fire. One is illustrated in figure 17.1, and figure 17.2 shows one in use. Traditionally made of iron by blacksmiths, they are a development of earlier wooden hooks, fashioned from a very hard wood such as yew or holly (Evans 1957, 68).

Fig. 17.1. Blacksmith-made pothook. Author's collection.

Fig. 17.2. The pothook in use. Drawing by the author.

French folklore calls it *le maître de la maison* (the master of the house), and in German-speaking lands it is the same—*der Hausherr*. It is the locus of the house spirit (Bächtold-Stäubli 1927–1942, vol. 4, 1274). As a symbol of ownership, the pothook form is used in the heraldry of the Holy Roman Empire, that is, in the arms of the Biedenfeld family of Hessen, the Komanski of Silesia, and the Schenk von Wettenstein of Swabia (Appulm 1994, 95, 131, 159). At weddings in the Eifel, the Rhineland, Westphalia, and Siebenbürgen, it was customary to use the pothook in the rites and ceremonies of weddings. For luck, the bride and groom made a threefold turn around the pothook, then the bride was swung at it three times (Bächtold-Stäubli 1927–1942, vol. 4, 1274). Pothooks have been used in pargeting in East Anglia to make patterns in the external plaster of house walls. A pothook swastika on an old house in Dunmow, Essex, is illustrated in figure 17.3.

Fig. 17.3. Pargeted pothook swastika, nineteenth century. Dunmow, Essex.

Blacksmiths use the same form for wall anchors; the often-reversed S shape is sometimes fashioned into an iron snake or crossed to make a swastika. Ella Mary Leather was told by the Rev. T. Oliver Minos that at Garway (Herefordshire) a blacksmith told him that they were made in that form to prevent the house from being struck by lightning (Leather 1912, 14–16). A serpentine wall anchor in Cambridge is shown in figure 17.4.

Fig. 17.4. Pothook wall anchor with serpents' heads, early nineteenth century. Kite Area, Cambridge.

Rudolf Koch called the pothook glyph "the wolf's tooth, or hanger" (Koch 1930; 83), and the wolf hook, or *Wolfsangel,* is an angularized form of the glyph with a crossbar. It represents a central European tool or weapon used to catch and torture wolves. Sir Flinders Petrie classified it under the rubric "spiral: whorl and S" (Petrie 1930; XXIX) (fig. 17.5).

Fig. 17.5. Curved pothook symbol

Runically, the pothook is the Anglo-Saxon yew rune *eoh* (Germanic *Eihwaz*), recalling the wood that some pothooks were made of anciently (Johnston 1912, 362–63; Pennick 1989b, 84; 1992b, 79–81, 158–59; 1999b, 56). Related to the *Wolfsangel* is the sign of the Vehmgericht, a secret society that existed in the later years of the Holy Roman Empire to perform summary executions of supposed miscreants. Its sigil was called the *Donnerbesen* (thunder broom), in this form a pothook-related glyph like an eight-armed swastika (another glyph called *Donnerbeson* is totally different) (fig. 17.6).

Fig. 17.6. The Donnerbesen, an eight-armed swastika

18. THE TREFOT

Best known in Great Britain as the three-legged emblem of the Isle of Man, the *trefot, treefoot,* or *triskele* is related to the *valknut.* Often taken to be a three-legged version of the swastika, it is a glyph in its own right (fig. 18.1).

Fig. 18.1. The trefot

Fig. 18.2. Double trefot sigil used by the German runemaster Marby. The Library of the European Tradition.

Sir Flinders Petrie lists the trefot among "triskele, dragons, nautilus," and shows curved forms from ancient artifacts from Pylos, Lycia, Syracuse, Schleswig-Holstein, Ireland, and France (Petrie 1930, VII). In the first half of the twentieth century, the German rune master Friedrich Bernhard Marby used the double trefot illustrated in figure 18.2 as one of his personal glyphs (Marby 1931, 83).

In heraldry this glyph is shown as three armored legs, as on the carving shown in figure 18.3, from the College of Arms in London,

Fig. 18.3. Heraldic trefot on the College of Arms, London

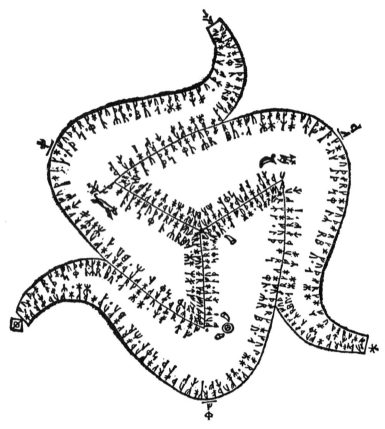

Fig. 18.4. Mid-seventeenth-century trefot-form runic calendar from Österbotten, Finland, "På bräde uti en Treefootz lijkness," from Olaf Rudbeck's *Atlantica*. The Library of the European Tradition.

described in heraldic terms as "three legs armed, conjoined at the fess point at the upper extremity of the thigh, flexed in a triangle, garnished and spurred." A woodcut in the second volume of Olaf Rudbeck's *Atlantica* depicts a mid-seventeenth-century runic calendar from Österbotten, Finland, "På bräde uti en Treefootz lijkness" (in the likeness of a treefoot) (fig. 18.4). The threefold year of the northern tradition fits this form admirably.

A related form, a circle with a skirl of three lines within it, is an element in Gothic art that was used for stonework, woodwork, leaded-glass windows, and in pargeting, as in the panel on a house wall in Saffron Walden, Essex, shown in figure 18.5.

Fig. 18.5. Trefot triquetra pargeting work of
the Gothic form, Saffron Walden, Essex

19. THE HORSESHOE

Horseshoes are part of the blacksmith's craft, iron forged and hammered into shape. It is a crescent shape, and so allied with the form of the crescent moon, and in rune lore, the second rune, *ur* (Von Zaborsky 1936, 52–53). As a luck bringer, a horseshoe is nailed on or above a door or window, or on a ship's mast (fig. 19.1). Even churches have borne horseshoes "to keep away the witches" (Johnston 1912, 157), and on mosques a horseshoe is said to signify the crescent (Whittick 1971, 257).

Fig. 19.1. A superannuated
horseshoe in its traditional
position as a door protector

Writing in 1894, George Day recalled, "At Ilford I saw a horse-shoe nailed to the door of a cow-house, and on asking the lad the reason, he replied, 'Why, to keep the wild horse away, to be sure'" (Day 1894, 77). In 1895 Frederick Thomas Elworthy noted that in Somerset horse-shoes were nailed to stable doors, hung up on the ceiling above horses, or put on the walls of cowhouses "to keep off the pixies" (Elworthy 1895, 217). Horseshoes have been used as stamps in pargeting work in East Anglia, as in the example at Thaxted, Essex, shown in figure 19.2. Folklore asserts that the horseshoe should appear with its horns point-ing upward; to set it the other way will result in one's luck running out (Villiers 1923, 92). Here the horseshow is seen as a container or recep-tacle of luck that operates according to gravity.

Fig. 19.2. Pargeting glyph made from horseshoes and riding crops, Thaxted, Essex

Roy Palmer notes that in Herefordshire and Worcestershire, when the horseshoe has its points upward, it is connected with the moon and, with its points downward, the Greek character *omega,* the final letter of that alphabet (Palmer 1992, 109). With the horns down this is the *ur* rune, where the sun sleeps at midwinter, the form of ancient stone burial chambers (Wirth 1931–1936, vol. 3, 259–88, pls. 74, 75; Von Zaborsky 1936, 54). Hence it is related to the glyph for wintertime and of course the other way up with its Roman letter equivalent, *U.* One theory of the origin of the horseshoe as an amulet is that it comes from the remnant of images of saints with the nimbus or halo, where the rest had faded away, leaving only the nimbus (Whittick 1971, 257).

As a sign of the horseman's craft, the horn buttons of the traditional Suffolk horseman's suit have the image of the shoed hoof with its seven nails (Tony Harvey, personal communication). Magnets are, of course, made from iron, and their customary form is the horseshoe magnet, which is a meaningful form for such a powerful artifact. Figure 19.3 shows a complex transference of imagery and meaning, in a cartouche on the remaining unrebuilt part of Holborn tube station, Kingsway, London, designed by Leslie W. Green and opened in 1906 (Leboff 2002, 82). This was the entrance to the offices of the British Electrical Federation Ltd., which used a glyph composed of a section of grooved tram rail in the form of a horseshoe magnet powering a wheel from the hub of which emerge lightning flashes. This is an instance of a new symbolic glyph being devised from traditional elements for a new purpose.

Fig. 19.3. Electrical emblem, tram rail horseshoe magnet and wheel, designed by Leslie W. Green, Kingsway, London, 1906

20. TOOLS AND CRAFT SYMBOLS

The hammer is the primary emblem of human craft, for it enables the materials of the world to be changed in form through the application of human skill and strength. There are a few hints in northern myth that Thor has aspects of blacksmithing among his attributes (fig. 20.1). The hammering of a smith on an anvil replicated thunder in the heavens, as noted by Saxo Grammatius in *Gesta Danorum* (XII, chapter 13, line 421).

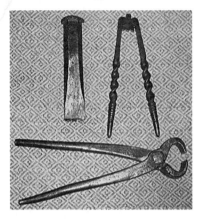

Fig. 20.1. Blacksmith-made tools. Author's collection.

The High Thunderer Thor wears the heavy belt, Meginjord, as do blacksmiths, and wields a heavy, short-handled hammer, Mjöllnir, "the Crusher." In his journey to Utgard, his servant is warned not to break the leg bones of his goats when they are killed, for when they are resurrected they will not walk properly. Ancient smiths used bellows of animal skin with the long leg bones as the tuyeres that supplied air to the furnace. If they were broken, then the furnace could not be fired. And in some places, temples of Thor had altars that were blocks of metal—anvils.

The hammer of Thor is a symbol of right orderliness struggling against the inchoate powers of dissolution and chaos. Small metal Thor's hammers were popular sacred symbols in the old North, worn around the neck on a cord, and they are made to this day. A twentieth-century one is shown in figure 20.2. The glyph appears in the landscape on ancient boundary stones, emphasizing their permanence in maintaining rightful property and authentic jurisdiction. Tenth-century hammer-shaped amulets from Östergotland and Scania in Sweden have

Fig. 20.2. Hammer of Thor with warding signs, England, twentieth century. Author's collection.

a glyph that can be interpreted as a stylized face of the god (Davidson 1993, 53–54). An Anglo-Saxon runestone found at Dover has an image that may represent the hammer of Thunor, the Anglo-Saxon version of Thor, though in outline shape it resembles some forms of a brooch of the same period, demonstrating the mutability of forms and their interpretation (fig. 20.3).

Fig. 20.3. Runestone from Dover, in hammer or anchor form. The Library of the European Tradition.

This glyph is called *ul* by Herman Wirth, who likens it with rock carvings a thousand years earlier (Wirth 1931–1936, vol. 7, 722, pl. 374, 2). The swastika is also known as Thórshamarr, as a glyph denoting the attributes of the god, lightning and thunder (Thorsson 1993, 14). Thor's hammer is linked with the Donnerbesen (thunder broom), a glyph prevalent in German folk art and part of the repertoire of patterns in brick-nogged timber-frame buildings in the region of Lippe in Germany (Von Zaborsky 1936, 112–13). In form the Donnerbesen is the same as the goose-feather brushes used in traditional bakeries to brush out the hot ashes from the stone on which the dough is placed to bake.

A related symbol is the double ax. It is a symbol nowadays most evocative of ancient Crete and used by some goddess worshippers as their glyph. Called the *labrys,* it has been the center of much speculation over its relationship with the labyrinth, another glyph associated with

Fig. 20.4. Twy-bill (double ax)

Crete. But in medieval England it was called the *twy-bill,* and to the learned this glyph was the *bipennis,* the two-edged ax of Tenedos, symbol of extreme severity (fig. 20.4).

Members of medieval craft guilds usually signified their places of work and their property by images of their main working tools. A 1636 cast-iron fireback by the Sussex iron master Richard Leonard illustrated in figure 20.5 shows the working tools of the caster of metals. As a hammerman he wields a hammer, and the fireback also shows his foundry, the wheelbarrow used for carrying the mold-making sand, and a fireback-within-a-fireback bearing his initials and a diamond.

Craftsmen's tombstones in Scotland of the seventeenth and eighteenth centuries frequently bear carvings depicting the tools of the trade. They appear along with the deceased's initials, a date, and sometimes emblems of mortality such as the skull and crossbones

Fig. 20.5. Fireback made by the Sussex iron master Richard Leonard in 1636. The Library of the European Tradition.

or an hourglass and perhaps a tradesman's personal sigil. Only two Scottish trades were allowed to use the crown in conjunction with their emblematic tools: the cordiners (shoemakers) and the hammermen, which covered all trades using the hammer. These two were the senior guilds of the Incorporated Trades in Scotland. Cordiners' memorials have an image of the craft's leather-cutting knife with a semicircular blade beneath the crown, while the crowned hammer is the glyph of the guild of hammermen. The type of hammer denotes the particular trade within the guild (Mair 1988, 131–35).

The anchor is a vital implement in travels on the sea, enabling a ship to be anchored at a particular place and no longer subject to the currents and tides. Forged from iron by anchor smiths, conventionally it appears in two forms. The older one resembles Irminsul and was one of the inspirations for wall anchors when brick building began and needed to be held together by iron. The more familiar anchor glyph has various forms, but its resemblance to the cross, and its literal meaning, made it into a Christian symbol of hope (figs. 20.6 and 20.7).

Figs. 20.6. and 20.7.
Anchors, older and later forms

The hammer and sickle as an emblem of work—symbolic of the craftsman and agricultural worker—seems to have originated in the French Second Empire, when they appeared on the coins of Napoléon III. Subsequently, together as a single glyph, the hammer and sickle was adopted as the glyph of communism (fig. 20.8).

Fig. 20.8. The hammer and sickle

In the Soviet Union the title Geroj Sotsialistitjeskoto Truda (Hero of Socialist Work) was awarded to civilian workers who had contributed to the greatness and glory of the USSR. Heroes of Socialist Work received the gold medal Serp i Molot, the hammer-and-sickle medal

(Hieronymussen and Strüwing 1967, 191–92). After the Soviet conquest of 1945, a related glyph was adopted by the Deutsche Demokratische Republik (Communist East Germany). It was the hammer and dividers (compasses), which was reminiscent of part of the Masonic glyph, the square and compasses. It went out of use when the Republik fell in 1989 (fig. 20.9).

Fig. 20.9. The emblem of the Deutsche Demokratische Republik (Communist East Germany)

The emblem of the masons' craft, the square and compasses, is a more familiar glyph, having been around much longer. Like the craftsmen's tools, it also appears on tombstones, not only in Scotland. The square and compasses emblem may be an indicator of the grave of a craftsman, but more probably marks the last resting place of a speculative Freemason. A Masonic stone dated 1923 in the east end of Peterborough Cathedral is shown in figure 20.10, along with the door-head of a Masonic building in Sheffield in figure 20.11. The door-head has a sun and moon, wreathed square and compasses, and wreathed level that all appear within the rays of a larger sunburst that of course follows the tradition of sun and doorway.

Because through human skill the world is altered by tools, they have a magical dimension. Iron in general is an apotropaic material, and edged tools are especially prized. An adage recorded by Frederick Thomas Elworthy tells us:

Fig. 20.10. Masonic stone in Peterborough Cathedral dated 1923

Fig. 20.11. Masonic emblems on a door-head, Sheffield

Hang up hooks and shears to scare
Hence the hag, who rides the mare,
Till they be all over wet
With the mire and the sweat.

(ELWORTHY 1895, 217)

This is the same function that the stable lad told George Day at Ilford, in the county of Essex of the horseshoe. Sickles and scythes are, like the horseshoe, emblematic of the moon, and we may come across images of tools pressed into plaster during the process of pargeting. The pargeted panel on a house in Great Sampford, Essex, shown in figure 20.12 has scissors marking out the corners of the panel in which a pattern of nine roses is molded.

Fig. 20.12. Pargeting emblem of nine roses with scissors at the corners, Great Sampford, Essex

21. THE *X, GYFU, DAEG,* AND *ING* GLYPHS

There are three closely related runic glyphs used in the traditional crafts and in building. They are *gyfu, daeg,* and *ing.* The rune *gyfu* is the *X* glyph that appears in most alphabets in the West, often with different phonetic meanings. Primarily, *X* is a sign of crossing out, of making a blockage. This glyph is often called St. Andrew's cross, though frequently the name is used in contexts where there is no reference to the saint. This cross, heraldically a saltire, is the glyph of the flag of Scotland, whose patron is St. Andrew. But the *X* glyph is also called the pagan cross, and it is said to be the sign of consecration in the elder faith in central and northern Europe. There is an East Anglian brickmaking tradition of marking bricks with the sign so they can be placed above doorways during building construction to turn away bad luck. Along with the pothook, the *X* glyph is a favorite of anchor smiths for walls. Another instance is the creation of the pattern by other things, as in the impressed tools in the pargeted wall in Thaxted, Essex, shown in figure 21.1, in crossed swords as a military sign, or the skull and crossbones that compose the death's head glyph.

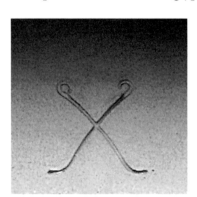

Fig. 21.1. Impressed tools in the pargeted wall, Thaxted, Essex

The Old English rune *daeg* is described in *The Old English Rune Poem* as "day, the Lord's message, dear to men." Some Anglo-Saxon sundials mark the beginning of the working day, 7:30 a.m., by a *daeg* rune (Jones 1991a, 15–16). Shutters and doors in the Netherlands and Frisia traditionally are painted with the *daeg* glyph. This signifies

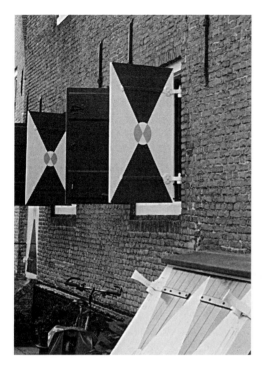

Fig. 21.2. Shutters painted with traditional *daeg* pattern in Middelburg, Zeeland, the Netherlands

their closing at night and their opening during the hours of daylight. Shutters displaying this glyph in a street in Middelburg, Zeeland, the Netherlands, are shown in figure 21.2.

Work on runes and related signs by Guido List and later Herman Wirth led Walter Propping in 1935 to call this sign *tag* (day) and link it with the Elder Futhark rune *dag* and the double ax or *twy-bill* (Wirth 1931–1936, vol. 1, 56; vol. 6, 556–73; Propping 1935, 144). Rune lore teaches that the *daeg* glyph signifies a stable balance between the opposites of light and darkness, opening and closing. As the door it allows entry of favorable things and keeps out the unwelcome. *Daeg* is made in traditional blacksmith work as a closure near the end of the piece, as in a wall anchor at Caister-On-Sea. This usage is very ancient, as it can be seen universally on medieval wrought-iron work, and on earlier metal artifacts recovered archaeologically from Anglo-Saxon and other old Germanic contexts. As well as on doors and shutters, the *daeg* glyph is painted or carved on doorposts and other uprights in a house, most notably in the traditional farmhouses of Ryedale and Eskdale in Yorkshire. From 1936 onward posts carved with this glyph have been called witch posts (Hayes and Rutter 1972, 87). Before then they were known as speer posts or heck posts from their location supporting the timber screen with seats next to the inglenook fireplace. The glyph carved very visibly on the post was made to protect the house and hearth against ill-wishing witchcraft.

There are two forms of the *ing* glyph, a closed, contained form shaped like a diamond in the playing card suit or a square stood on its corner, and an open form with spreading lines promising infinite expansion (fig. 21.3).

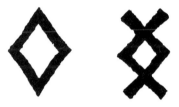

Fig. 21.3. *Ing* rune, outgoing form (left) and inward form (right)

In the *Old English Rune Poem,* the rune *ing* stands for the god first seen by folk among the East Danes, who then went over the waves. Geometrically, it can be presented as an Egyptian diamond, that is, a figure measuring eight units high by six wide that has a circumference that measures twenty units. Seen as four right-angled Pythagorean triangles back to back, it appeared in eighteenth-century Masonic usage, as the basis for some British road and rail signs of the nineteenth century, and as an early railway trademark. Another version can be two equilateral triangles, base to base, as in the heraldic escutcheon of a woman. Equally, it can be a square standing on its corner.

The fundamental geometry of brickwork lends itself to the creation of *ing* patterns and the related *Godsoog.* On the clock tower at Fenstanton, Old Huntingdonshire, shown in figure 21.4, is a single enclosed-form *ing* in contrasting brickwork. The glyph can be expanded to cover the whole surface as diaper work (repeated pattern of squares) or made into a columnar form as in the house in Bury St. Edmunds, Suffolk, shown in figure 21.5.

Fig. 21.4. Inward form of *ing* rune in brickwork on a clock tower at Fenstanton, Old Huntingdonshire

Fig. 21.5. Expansive *ing* rune in contrasting-colored bricks. Tower Cottage, Bury St. Edmunds, Suffolk.

Fig. 21.6. Elongated *ing* rune on a pargeted panel, Thaxted, Essex

In pargeting the glyph may alter its relative dimensions to fit, as in the panel from Thaxted, Essex, shown in figure 21.6. Rarely, it is carved in brick, as in the *ing* containing a heart in King's Lynn, Norfolk, shown in figure 21.7, which is said to mark the place where the heart of a woman who was burned at the stake exploded and hit the wall.

Fig. 21.7. *Ing* with heart, marking the point where a heart exploding from the body of a woman being burned at the stake for petty treason hit the wall, King's Lynn, Norfolk

Another form approaches the square, as in the glyphs in Lowestoft flanking the date of construction surmounting the door (fig. 21.8, left). As a square diamond, it is one form employed in drawing magical talismans, as the Bavarian example (fig. 21.8, right).

Fig. 21.8. (Left) *ing* square pargeted panels, Lowestoft
(right) *ing*-pattern door, Bavaria, Germany

The Icelandic diagram in figure 21.9 is an insigil that invokes the power of the ancient Hebrew warrior Joshua. Insigils are glyphs composed of a number of characters or signs enclosed in a circle or square. As a double square, the *ing* is a door pattern made in the carpentry in traditional houses in central Europe. And another version is used

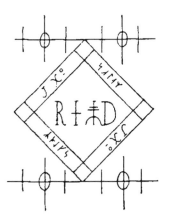

Fig. 21.9. Square form insigil of Joshua, Iceland, collected by Óláfur Davídsson, 1903. The Library of the European Tradition.

in pargeting in eastern England, where small square diamond stamps are arranged to make a large design arrayed in the same shape. In this instance the glyph parallels the checkerboard.

22. THE HEXFLOWER

In sacred geometry the division of the circle into six by its radius can be developed further by joining up the points with straight lines to make the hexagram or by drawing arcs of the same radius across the circle, creating a six-petaled form called the hexflower (fig. 22.1).

Fig. 22.1. Hexflower

Among other meanings, in ancient times it was an emblem of the goddess Juno, and it appears on many Roman altars and tombs, perhaps in that context. It is a glyph used in European folk art, such as the cutouts on the shutters in Cambridge shown in figure 22.2, and it is celebrated among the hex signs in the traditional building of people of German descent in Pennsylvania, the Pennsylvania Dutch (from *Deutsch,* meaning "German").

Fig. 22.2. Hexflower cutouts on window shutters, Cambridge

An American hex sign with this glyph is shown in figure 22.3, its petals alternating with hearts. In Pennsylvania this sign is often called the rosette, though it has six petals, not five as does the rose. This is a good luck sign for love and romance.

Fig. 22.3. Hex pattern, Pennsylvania

There are other hex signs that are not geometric, but sport other patterns such as oak leaves for strength; the *Distelfink* (goldfinch), a bird that brings good luck; twin unicorns as a sign of peace and contentment; and the word *Wilkommen* for hospitality. Sometimes this six-petaled glyph is not separate from the customary circles drawn around it, but the petals are depicted like spokes in a wheel, and it merges with the glyphs of the six-spoked wheel and the six-pointed star in a circle (fig. 22.4). In another design, the hexflower merges with hexagonal patterns made in brush strokes, as in the pattern from Slovakia shown in figure 22.5.

Fig. 22.4. Six-spoked hexflower wheel

Fig. 22.5. Hexagonal glyph, house- and furniture-painting design, Slovakia

23. WOVEN PATTERNS

The patterns that all things make are perceived by humans as the cosmic order. They appear everywhere we care to look, and all human makings conform to these patterns. They are described poetically in myths and legends of creation. Two of the most ancient crafts of humankind are weaving and potting, and both of them serve as metaphors for the human condition (fig. 23.1).

Fig. 23.1. Knotted serpent rope, from a medieval engraving. The Library of the European Tradition.

The ancient poets described the multiple strands of interwoven existence in terms of a symbolic cloth, woven by the powers that we call fate or destiny. Human existence is envisaged as part of a great interweaving pattern, known in the northern tradition as the web of wyrd. Fortune and destiny are symbolized as weaving in the Old English word *gewaef,* as in the text, *"Me that wyrd gewæf"* (wyrd wove me that; that is my lot, or place, or fate, in life). The weavers of the fabric are the Three Fates, personifications of three states that we perceive to be the process that is existence. There are three because this process can be said to consist of formation, becoming, and dissolution. Images of weaving appear in pargeting work in eastern England, representing the fabric of the world, as on the house in Bury St. Edmunds, Suffolk, shown in figure 23.2.

The oldest recorded appearance of these shapers of becoming was in ancient Greece, where they were described as the Moirai, daughters of the darkness of night. Writing around 850 BCE, Hesiod named them "Clotho, Lachesis, and Atropos, who give people at their birth both ill and good." Orpheus, the prophet of the religion of Dionysos, spoke of "the Moirai in white raiment." Devotees of the Orphic faith symbolized the Moirai with three phases of the moon: waxing, full, and waning. Clotho spins the thread of life, Lachesis measures it, and Atropos cuts it. Human life is fragile and sometimes hangs by a thread. How the thread

Fig. 23.2. Pargeted panels on a house in Bury St. Edmunds,
Suffolk, with weaving patterns

of life is spun, what colors and textures it possesses, determines our
individual character and life experience. Our parentage, our genetics,
and our birth environment are symbolized by the kind of thread spun
by Clotho. Composed of many fibers, the complex nature of the thread
determines in great measure how life progresses. She spins it by means
of the rotating spindle whose motion imitates the spinning nights and
days of our existence. To use this given thread of existence well in the
creative acceptance of life is the ideal of the ancient philosophers, as in
the Stoic tradition of the second-century CE Roman Emperor Marcus
Aurelius Antoninus, who advised, "Offer yourself wholeheartedly to
Clotho, let her spin your thread of whatever material she will."

Lachesis symbolizes the interweaving of one's personal thread with all the other strands of life and the world. To the Greeks she was the measurer of the span of life. In the northern tradition, where the three Weird Sisters or Norns parallel the Greek Moirai, Lachesis is Verdandi, who weaves the threads into the fabric of life, fashioning the web of wyrd. The warp of her weaving signifies the passing of time and the appearance of events, while the weft denotes the actions of the individual interacting with it. The last of the Moirai is Atropos, known in the North in her Weird Sister form as Skuld. She terminates the individual's thread of life, cutting it with her shears or ripping it apart. The prime emblem of the web of wyrd is the seamless textile, symbolized in traditional Hindu dress, fabric uncut and unfitted; the legendary seamless garment of Jesus; and the smocks of traditional seamstresses in Great Britain and Scandinavia. For existence is not composed of a digital assemblage of separate moments, but it is a seamless flow of process, the threads of which are as but currents in a river, tides in a sea, or the blowing of the winds.

24. PLAITS AND KNOTS

Knots are a recognized way to tie up things magically as well as physically, and they are the means by which knitted garments are made. A Cambridgeshire courting custom uses a true lover's knot plaited from straw. The suitor gives his potential wife a straw plait, and if she wears it later pinned to her dress on the right side, it is a sign of rejection. If to the left, by the heart, with the ears of corn pointing right, it is a sign of acceptance (Porter 1969, 1–2). Binding spells are intended to be the equivalent of physical knots, nets, and ropes tying up the designated target. Many religious traditions of the world use a knotted cord or string of beads with knots as an aid to concentration in devotional exercises. They go under various names, but are called rosaries in English, after the Christian version. Rosaries exist in various forms as part of the Buddhist, Christian, Mohammedan, and Sikh religions. European folklore records that interlacing patterns—knots—serve to bind up bad luck and ward off the causes of bad luck. Such knots serve to enclose and bind the harmful influences, bringing them to a full stop (Pennick

Fig. 24.1. Six-sword lock
or knot, English traditional
longsword dance, Benwick,
Cambridgeshire

1989b, 180–88). In mythology harmful powerful beings are captured and bound by the powers of right orderliness. Northern tradition writings (*Gylfaginning* 34, 51) tell of the binding of the Fenris-Wolf and Loki, and Christian eschatology in the book of Revelations (20:1–3) describes the bondage of the devil in chains for a thousand years. A photograph of the bound devil on a building in York appears in Part I (page 5). Knots made in rope, cord, and netting for practical and magical purposes, as well as women's hair braiding, and interlaces made during performances such as sword dancing, are transitory, and there are few surviving examples from ancient times. The sword dancers shown in figure 24.1 have just made a knot and are holding it up.

The pentagrammic knot of swords in figure 24.2 comes from the cover of the first volume of Cecil J. Sharp's *The Sword Dances of*

Fig. 24.2. Pentagrammic five-
sword lock. Illustration from
the cover of volume 1 of Cecil
J. Sharp's *The Sword Dances of
Northern England*. The Library of
the European Tradition.

Northern England. Making *troll-knutar* (troll knots or cats' cradles) from string is one practice that has survived from a northern circumpolar tradition of binding magic linked to shamanic practices.

The picture in figure 24.3 shows a wise woman in Sweden, around 1920, making a troll knot. In more durable materials, knots and interlaces were used by Roman mosaic makers, and later, Irish craft workers made them their own in metalwork, wood carving, leather, and illuminated manuscripts. Interlaced beasts appeared in Allemannic culture around the same time and were later brought to a fine art in Scandinavia and Great Britain.

Fig. 24.3. Wise woman making a troll knot, Sweden, circa 1920. The Library of the European Tradition.

The simplest interlaced knot, the fourfold loop, survives on a memorial stone on the Baltic island of Gotland (for Havor II, Habingo Parish). It dates from between 400 and 600 CE (Nylén and Lamm 1981, 39). It appears also on bracteates from Denmark of roughly the same date (Wirth 1931–1936, vol. 8, pl. 424, fig. 1b; pl. 427, fig. 7b) and in a squared-off version on the Andreas cross on the Isle of Man. Early Lombardic and Romanesque churches in Germany, Switzerland, and Italy have the sign carved in stone on column capitals, fonts, and stone screens, where they appear among other interlaced patterns. In Sweden this knot is called a *Sankt Hans vapen,* and in Finland and Estonia a *hannunvaakuna* (Strygell 1974, 46), though it is clearly pre-Christian in origin. A Sankt Hans vapen is illustrated in figure 24.4 on a Sámi shaman's drum, as illustrated in Johannes Schefferus's *Lapponia* (1673), and another is shown in figure 24.5. This simple sigil appeared

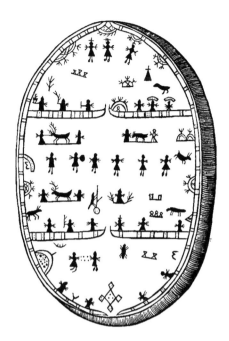

Fig. 24.4. Lappish shaman's drum with glyphs including a rectilinear version of a Sankt Hans vapen. From Johannes Schefferus's *Lapponia*. The Library of the European Tradition.

Fig. 24.5. Sankt Hans vapen

Fig. 24.6. Drawing by the author of the stonework of the transept window of William Richard Lethaby's church at Brockhampton, Herefordshire, following the pattern of a Sankt Hans vapen and the houses of heaven

in Great Britain in medieval graffiti, as at Cowlinge in Suffolk (e.g., Pritchard 1967, 133), and in 1901, William Richard Lethaby used the pattern for the tracery of the north transept window in his symbolic church at Brockhampton, Herefordshire (Mason 2001, 14), illustrated here in figure 24.6.

Fig. 24.7 Sigil of the nameless art.
Painting by the author, 1994.

Figure 24.7 shows the sigil of the nameless art, the name given to traditional natural magic in East Anglia (eastern England) (Pennick 1995b, 117). A sigil used in traditional furniture painting in Austria is shown in figure 24.8.

Fig. 24.8. Knot from Austrian
traditional furniture painting

In the introduction I mentioned the principle of spectacle or the fetishism of the object, where observers concentrate on a particular part of an ensemble, ignoring the context in which it is found. As an example of this tendency, commentators on the swastika are attracted by the particular sort of knot that academics call the swastika pelta. Because the swastika pattern is part of the tighter versions of these knots, it is assumed that it is the major characteristic, and thus they are classified among swastikas, fylfots, and gammadions rather than among decorative and magical knots, where taxonomy would naturally place them. In his 1930 classification of ancient signs, Sir Flinders Petrie puts this sign under the rubric "twists" of the subgroup "double links" (Petrie 1930, XLII, E2, E4–6, E21, E28, E29), not under "swastika" (Petrie 1930, LXIX, LXX). The name *swastika pelta,* bringing words from Sanskrit and Latin together to make a scientific-sounding descriptor, is relatively recent. Because the knot was not seen as a swastika but as a twist in 1930, it is possible that a heightened awareness to swastikas in general came about as the result of the Nazis, making people view this knot in a new way, thereby giving rise to a new academic name that emphasizes only this component of the design. *Pelta* means "shield," as in the Scandinavian vapen description of knots, and the English descriptor *shield knot* is immediately intelligible, also it does not carry the value judgment that the sign is a form of swastika (fig. 24.9).

Fig. 24.9. Shield knot with dots of the nine-dot pattern

With a central cross-loop, the fourfold loop was used on English clog almanacs as the sigil of All Saints' Day, November 1 (e.g., Schnippel 1926, pls. II and III). It is the sigil for Samhain in the present-day pagan culture (Pennick 1990c, 35, figs. 8, 13, 26, 35). In 1947 a variant of this knot was described on a wooden vessel from Setesdal in Norway and called *valknute* (Weiser-Aal 1947, 126). The name *valknute, valknut,* or *valnkútr* is more commonly used for the three interlaced equilateral triangles that were carved on some memorial stones on Gotland and on rings and other Viking-age metalwork. It is associated with the Norse god Odin as "the knot of the slain" (Thorsson 1984, 107; 1993, 11; Aswynn 1988, 153–54).

Thorsson connects this glyph with the triquetra, used in Christian symbolism to denote the three deities in one that compose the godhead. The triquetra is drawn with a single line, making a single threefold loop, related more closely to the Sankt Hans vapen than to the triangular form shown in figure 24.10, which is three separate equilateral triangles interlaced (Thorsson 1993, 11). A different form of triangular knot, with a superimposed cross, is known as *Sankt Bengt's vapen*

Fig. 24.10. The valknut

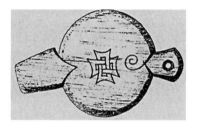

Fig. 24.11. Knot carved on oar-hole cover on the Viking-age Gokstad ship. The Library of the European Tradition.

(Strygell 1974, 46), while another version, shown in figure 24.11, was found as a protective glyph on the wooden oar-hole covers of a Viking-age ship excavated at Gokstad farm in Sandefjord, Norway.

Fig. 24.12. The Godsoog

A related version of the Sankt Hans vapen is the Dutch Godsoog (God's eye), figure 24.12. This glyph is said to signify the all-seeing eye of God. Knitted as part of the pattern of fishermen's ganseys, it is said to look after men in strange ports so that they will not go astray. Over the bar in the inns they frequented in the fishing ports was set the Godsoog, emphasized by the accompanying motto, "God sees you" (Van der Klift-Tellegen 1987, 19, 34–35). Dutch fishermen referred to ganseys bearing this pattern as English sweaters: garments knitted in stockinette except for the Godsoog motif on the front. However, as with many glyphs, the name and explanatory story is not universal, for at Urk, a town that was once an island in the Zuider Zee, the same pattern is called the flower.

Complex knotwork or interlacing is characteristic of what is called Celtic art, for the most stunning examples of this art form are found in Wales, Scotland, and Ireland (e.g., Romilly Allen 1904; Bryce 1989; Pennick 1997a), though it is a feature of Christian art as far away as Armenia and Ethiopia. The interlaced pattern shown in figure 24.13 on the ninth-century royal cross stored in Llantwit Major church is a particularly fine example of Welsh art, though the cross has been battered by the steel chairs stacked against it.

Fig. 24.13. Shaft of cross at Llantwit Major, Wales, showing knotwork

The labyrinth is also a sort of knot, and in addition to those large enough to dance or walk in, smaller ones are used as apotropaic devices in connection with doors and entrances, said to trap sprites bent on mischief inside them. Of course, the oldest known labyrinths are scribed and carved in stone or hammered into coins. But glyphs in these media are the most likely to remain when the people, cultures, and customs of a place and era are long since obliterated. Legends of labyrinths tell of them as symbols of binding and enclosure of bad luck and the promotion of good fortune.

Folklore from Great Britain, Scandinavia, and German-speaking countries recounts stories of labyrinths binding the *smågubbar* (gremlins), controlling the wind, warding off storms, keeping sheep safe from wolves, and facilitating the cure of mental illness (Pennick 1990a, 44–48). A labyrinth is the motif on the shield of Graitschen in Germany, shown in figure 24.14, emphasizing its defensive quality.

The labyrinth is not fixed in form, but many variants are possible. A new design that I did is shown in figure 24.15. Labyrinths large

Fig. 24.14. Escutcheon of the township of Graitschen, Germany, with the local labyrinth depicted

Fig. 24.15. New labyrinth design by the author

enough to dance through are more celebrated, because since the 1980s there has been a renaissance of labyrinth construction, in which I have played my part, among others constructing one of the first new stone labyrinths in North America in 1986. An outdoor 1993 labyrinth built to my original design in a village near Stuttgart, Germany, is shown in figure 24.16. Its pattern is based on the German and Baltic form, where there is an entrance and an exit, not a dead-end at the center.

Fig. 24.16. Heart-shaped pavement labyrinth designed by the author for a private garden near Stuttgart, Germany

Another recent pavement labyrinth in the forecourt of St. Severin's church in Cologne, Germany, and guarding the entrance, takes the Christian labyrinth pattern in an octagonal shape (fig. 24.17). This shape is derived from the medieval labyrinths in the cathedrals at Amiens and St. Quentin, France, of 1288 and 1495, respectively (Pennick 1984b, 26–28).

Fig. 24.17. Octagonal pavement labyrinth in the forecourt of the church of St. Severin, Cologne, Germany

A magical threshold, doorway, stile, and field-gate blocker called the *Schratterlgatterl* is used in southern Germany, the Tyrol, and the Swiss Alps. It is interwoven from split fir wood and is the physical version of drawn and carved binding knots. Various parts of Great Britain have the custom of making similar temporary patterns on the threshold or hearthstone in order to bring good luck and ward off harm. Most of them are knot-form or binding patterns. In 1912, Sydney R. Jones noted, "Villagers throughout the north of England make a practice of sanding the steps to doorways. It is an odd custom, many years old, which still survives. The stone step is run over with water, partly dried, and to the damp surface is applied dry sand or sandstone. Varied are the patterns that are worked on risers and treads" (Jones 1912, 114, 116). In Scotland, Cheshire, East Anglia, and southwestern England, the patterns may be drawn with chalk, pipe clay, or sand (Canney 1926, 13). There is a pattern seemingly local to the town of Cambridge, called the Cambridge box (Pennick 2006b, 14). An example is illustrated in figure 24.18.

In Newmarket and Cambridge, a continuous loop pattern drawn around the edges of floors in stables and outhouses is called the running eight. Drawn in an unbroken movement, it is made without

Fig. 24.18. Cambridge box, traditional threshold pattern,
drawn in chalk

removing the hand during the process. This temporary pattern appears in permanent form in flooring made from traditional materials—bones, cobbles, bricks, and tiles—and in some places it is related to patterns in brickwork and clothing (Van der Klift-Tellegen 1987, 36–38). The patterns of East Anglian bit mats (rag rugs) often have a diamond in the center, a border, and triangles at the corners. Bit mats are made from material from worn-out old clothes cut into strips and attached to a fabric base (Dixon 1981, 46–47). These patterns also resemble some of the boxes or panels made in pargeting. They are not restricted to one medium; there is a continuum in their use.

25. STRAW PLAITS

The name corn dolly is used now to describe any of the many forms of straw plaiting. This use of word *dolly,* like many descriptors, is relatively recent, and was not in general use until after World War II. Its origin can be traced to a meeting of the Folk-Lore Society in London on Wednesday, February 20, 1901, when "Mrs. Gomme exhibited and presented to the society a Kirn Maiden or Dolly, copied by Miss Swan from those made at Duns in Berwickshire" (Gomme 1901, 11, 215–216). In a letter to Gomme, Miss Swan wrote, "I am sure that there was a good-luck superstition attached to the making and preserving of it, although it was not much talked about. The Kirn I sent you, though a modern dolly, is a faithful reproduction of those I have seen and helped to dress 'lang syne'" (Gomme 1901, 1, 215–16). This dolly was a copy, not an actual kirn maiden used in harvest rites and ceremonies. Earlier, straw plaits had other names; for example, William Hone, discussing the Norfolk harvest ceremonies, remarks, "Sometimes a sort of kern baby is placed on the top at the front of the load" (Hone 1827, vol. 2, 1166). Papers and reports in *Folk-Lore* on the subject following the Gomme article until World War II called corn plaits by their actual names, for example, necks from Cornwall and Devon, and kern babies from Hereford and Long Crendon, Buckinghamshire (*Folk-Lore* XXII, March 1911, 1) (fig. 25.1). Once the generic word *dolly* became the norm, it was analyzed etymologically as meaning the same as *idol* by Frazerian theorists (e.g., Evans 1965, 214; Butcher 1972, 463) and assumed thereby to be a goddess-worshipping woman's craft, contrary

Fig. 25.1. Straw plait, Shropshire, a border fan. Author's collection.

to the historical documentation. This assumption has led to its expansion into a new area, to be accepted also as a contemporary goddess-worshippers' emblem.

26. THE PENTAGRAM

Variously called by some the pentacle, pantacle, pentangle, pentagramma, flaming star, remphan, Solomon's seal, druid's foot, and *Drudenfuss,* this glyph is closely associated with magic (fig. 26.1). In his compendious 1930 work on glyphs, *Decorative Patterns of the Ancient World,* Sir Flinders Petrie illustrates ancient pentagrams from Cappadocia, Lombardy, and Cuma, dated before the year 700 CE (Petrie 1930, XLVIII, B9, B23, B44). Medieval and later folk magic ascribes the pentagram a protective power. It appears in the floor mosaic inside the entrance to St. Marco's Cathedral in Venice, Italy, (fig. 26.2) and, more generally, as a threshold pattern.

Fig. 26.1. The pentagram

Fig. 26.2. Disguised threshold pentagram just inside
the main entrance of the Cathedral of St. Marco, Venice, Italy

In his *Faust,* Johann Wolfgang von Goethe tells how Mephistopheles can enter Faust's place despite the "druid's foot" traced on the threshold. Mephistopheles gains entry because the *Drudenfuss* at the entrance has not been drawn properly: the lines are not as perfect as they ought to be; the outer angle is incomplete. The use of the pentagram as a threshold glyph may be referred to in one of the many versions of the English traditional counting song known as "The Twelve Apostles":

> *. . . Four for the Gospel makers,*
> *Five for the symbol at your door.*
> *Six for the six proud walkers . . .*

Lucy Broadwood and J. A. Fuller Maitland interpret this "five for the symbol" as signifying the pentagram (Broadwood and Maitland 1893, 154–59). In Freemasonry it has appeared as a symbolic glyph, as in William Hutchinson's *The Spirit of Masonry* (published in 1795) (Cooper 2006, 117). A 1641 sigil of the Scottish Freemason Sir Robert Moray is said to be the first known usage of the pentagram in that context. It is an interlaced

Fig. 26.3. The seal of Solomon. The Library of the European Tradition.

Fig. 26.4. Pentacle of Athanasius Kircher with pantacle enclosed within heptagram and empowered with sacred names. The Library of the European Tradition.

Fig. 26.5. Pentagrammic glyph on Victorian coal-hole cover, Castle Street, Cambridge

pentagram surrounded by Greek characters spelling *agapā*. In Masonic usage it signified the "five points of fellowship," but it has declined in usage in more recent times (Cooper 2006, 120–21). In Victorian times it was used as either a decorative or protective glyph on some pavement coal-hole covers. One from Cambridge is shown in figure 26.5.

The pentagram has an important place in sacred geometry because the fivefold division of the circle is the starting point for the proportion known as the golden section or golden cut. This is a proportion that exists between two measurable quantities of any sort when the ratio between the larger and smaller one is equal to the ratio between the sum of the two and the larger one. Geometrically, it is the ratio in the pentagram between the side of the inner pentagon and its extension into the pentagram, a ratio of 1:1.618, mathematically symbolized by the Greek glyph Φ. In any increasing progression or series of terms with Φ as the ratio between two successive terms, each term is equal to the sum of the two preceding ones. Usually implicit rather than overt, the fivefold pattern has appeared as itself in a few instances in medieval and Renaissance architecture. A pentagram as the centerpiece of a medieval rose window in Paderborn Cathedral in Germany is shown in figure 26.6.

As the pentagon it has been used more often in architecture and military engineering. A design for a pentagonal building was published by Italian Renaissance architect Sebastiano Serlio in his influential works (Pennick 2005b, 65). The pentagon was a favorite form for the engineers of sixteenth- and seventeenth-century fortresses, and in the twentieth century the headquarters of the United States military in Washington was built in the form of a vast pentagon, bearing the same name with the definitive article, *the* Pentagon.

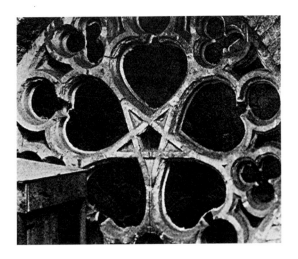

Fig. 26.6. Rose window, Paderborn Cathedral, Germany, with pentagram center. The Library of the European Tradition.

27. THE HEXAGRAM

The hexagram (fig. 27.1) is composed of two overlapping equilateral triangles. It signifies the union of the four elements, whose customary glyphs are shown in figure 27.2.

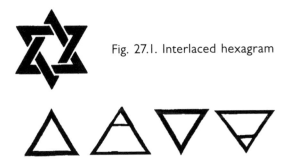

Fig. 27.1. Interlaced hexagram

Fig. 27.2. Sigils of the four elements of European traditional spirituality. Left to right: fire, air, earth, water.

The upright triangle also signifies male energy, and the opposite way round, female. Combined, we have the unity of opposites, which is a symbol of god, unifying the world above and the world below. The weathered Masonic stone at Harwich, Essex, shown in figure 27.3, has the hexagram. The Hebrew name for the sign, Magen David, means "shield of David," the word *shield* indicating its apotropaic and magical uses in warding off harmful influences. But it is not an exclusively

Fig. 27.3. Stone carved with a hexagram on a Masonic
building in Harwich, Essex

Jewish glyph, as it has a long history in pagan, Christian, and Masonic contexts too.

In the eighth and ninth centuries, the authorities in Mohammedan countries compelled Jews and Christians to wear distinctive dress to mark them out as unbelievers. Following the Muslim example, Jews were compelled to wear the Jewish badge by the Christian authorities in Europe. It was instituted by the fourth Lateran Council of the Roman Catholic Church in 1215. Its purpose was to prevent sexual contact between Jews and Christians (Unterman 1991, 32). The cloth badge was sewn onto the outer garments, and women were compelled to wear a distinctive hat or scarf, making Jews stand out from other people. The Jewish badge was a convenient means of persecution, which, in the twentieth century, led to the Star of David becoming almost exclusively a Jewish sign. When the German army conquered Poland in 1939, the Nazis forced Jews to wear a yellow Magen David, often with the word *Jude* written on it. Beginning in Poland, soon it was extended throughout Nazi-occupied Europe and served to label those who were to be persecuted. When the British military was forced in 1947 to retreat from Palestine by Zionist insurgents, the resulting state of Israel adopted the Magen David as the national emblem. Both of these usages subsequently led to the sign being largely abandoned in non-Jewish usage.

28. THE CHECKER

Weavers can create all manner of distinct patterns by selecting the threads during the weaving process. The allegory of the web of wyrd as the patterns of our own lives is based on this faculty, and similar metaphors for existence come from the randomness of divination and games. Life is fragile, and we never know which way those lucky dice are going to roll; life can be like snakes and ladders; we can be rolling on the wheel of fortune, having our ups and downs, or lead a checkered existence (fig. 28.1).

Fig. 28.1. *Ing* rune and double five-by-five checker pattern from Austrian traditional furniture painting. Drawing by the author.

Masonic symbology teaches that the checkered pavement, a tessela-tion of alternate black and white squares, signifies the world's nature, light and dark. It is another way of expressing the law of the unity of opposites symbolized in the Chinese yin and yang glyph. The check-erboard was used as a means of calculation and accounting in medieval times, as the British government official called the chancellor of the exchequer still recalls. The chessboard is the gaming version of this glyph, on which the playing pieces move. (The British name for the game of checkers is draughts.) Chess is said to have been devised by the Brahman sage Sissa at the court of King Balhait in ancient India as a means to cultivate knowledge, personal judgment, and anticipation in any circumstance, expressing all the principles of justice and acting as an ideal training in the art of war. The flag of the Knights Templar, Beauséant, was a checker of black and white, a symbol of order in the world. A thirteenth-century tomb slab from the Dominican House of Friars at Bangor, Wales, discovered in 1899, had a floriated cross whose staff was overlain by a four-by-four checker pattern whose alternate squares were inlaid in white metal (Hughes and North 1924, 199–200). A drawing made at the time is shown in figure 28.2.

Fig. 28.2. Four-by-four checker on a medieval tomb slab found in 1899 at the site of the Dominican House of Friars in Bangor, Wales. The Library of the European Tradition.

Heraldically, the red-and-white checker is the national glyph for Croatia. A pattern in Austrian traditional furniture painting is the *ing* rune overlain by checker patterns. This pattern is five squares by five, as is the Gothic example designed by the Arts and Crafts architect Edward Schroeder Prior on Henry Martyn Hall in Cambridge (fig. 28.3).

Fig. 28.3. Virtual five-by-five checker pattern in a Gothic arch on Henry Martyn Hall, Cambridge, one of Edward Schroeder Prior's symbolic Arts and Crafts masterpieces

This emblem was adopted in the twentieth century by car racing as the checkered flag used to signal the winner, so the image of the checker in play and combat was carried on in a new form. During the twentieth century, the checker was also adopted by police forces in Great Britain as a symbol of law and order.

29. HOUSE MARKS, CRAFTSMEN'S MARKS, AND SIGILS

The basic principle of ownership is symbolized in the runes by the glyph called *othala* in the Elder Futhark and *ethel* in the Old English runes, as described in *The Old English Rune Poem*. There, it is manifested as "Home is beloved of all humans," signifying each individual's inalienable right to his or her ancestral land and ancestral heritage. Traditional common law in northern Europe asserts the right of family land: it is eternal property, handed on through the generations; it cannot be sold and bought. In the Frisian language, this glyph is called *eeyen-eerde,* meaning "own earth" or "own land." Two alternative versions, one angular and one rounded, are illustrated in figures 29.1 and 29.2.

In the European tradition, makers of things are identified by their particular personal glyphs. Ancient weapons and armor bear their

Fig. 29.1. Ethel rune,* rectilinear form, signifying immutable ancestral property

Fig. 29.2. Ethel rune, round form, as adopted by pressure groups for colored ribbon campaigns (e.g., green for Sínn Féin, white for antiwar, pink for breast-cancer charity, blue and yellow for independence for East Anglia, etc.)

Ethel is the Anglo-Saxon name for this rune, *othala* is the old Germanic name for it, and *eeyen-eerde* is the Frisian language.

Fig. 29.3. Cast-iron fireback from Penshurst, Kent, with maker's marks, a version of the *ing* rune. The Library of the European Tradition.

makers' marks, as do metal castings such as bells and firebacks. The sixteenth-century cast-iron fireback from Penshurst, Kent, shown in figure 29.3, has a version of the *ing* rune on it, the founder's marks.

Worked stones in buildings sometimes bear visible marks carved there by stonemasons. Each mason had his own mark, given to him when he became an apprentice of the craft. This remained with him through his whole working life and was used to identify his work. Masons' marks are among the longest lasting of craftsmens' marks, but stonemasonry is by no means the only context in which such marks are used (fig. 29.4).

Fig. 29.4. Typical medieval masons' marks from England and Germany. Drawing by the author.

Rudolf Koch noted, "House-marks were, at first, private signs of peasant proprietors, and their use was originally confined to their holdings, all moveable property upon which was distinguished by the holdings-mark" (Koch 1930, 76). These holdings marks were used in many ways. They were ploughed into the strips of fields to identify which family had been allotted that rig that year. The rigs were allotted by drawing sticks marked with the house mark (fig. 29.5). In Scotland this is called *run-rig*. They were punched into timber floated downriver, which could be identified from its mark when it arrived at its destination. Marks were snipped into the ears of livestock, in the feet of web-footed birds, and on the bills of swans. They were clipped in the coats of horses, marked in tiver* on the fleeces of sheep, and branded on cattle. The glyphs were embroidered on clothes, woven into cloth, and used as watermarks in papermaking. The marks appeared on all tools, utensils, boats, carts, wagons, and sledges (Koch 1930, 76).

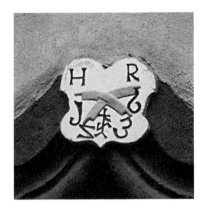

Fig. 29.5. House mark, initials and tools over a door at Wildberg, Germany, 1653

Koch showed how the mark of an individual might be handed down in the male line to his son and successive generations, each modified in a particular way, yet still identifiable as a family mark (Koch 1930, 85–89). Countless individual marks have been used across Europe in the past, and many are in use today (fig. 29.6). Old ones have been documented by local researchers. For example, in 1964, F. A. Girling listed 120 owners' marks, dating from the fourteenth to the seventeenth centuries, in Suffolk alone (Girling 1964, 122–26, figs. 18–22).

---

*Colored clay-based paint used to mark sheep.

Fig. 29.6. Escutcheon with house mark, Norwich, Norfolk

Many medieval merchants' marks are based on the sigil of Mercury, god of trade and business—the sign of Hermes, shown in figure 29.7. When Roman numerals were superseded by Arabic numerals from the fifteenth century, the number *4* was not written like this. But when the number *4* took on this form and became the predominant meaning of the glyph, then the original sign went into decline. The preference for the open-topped *4* in some places may have evolved as a means of distinguishing the Hermetic sigil from the numeral. The medieval German merchant's mark belonging to Peter Vischer shown in figure 29.8 is a double sign of Hermes.

Fig. 29.7. The sign of Hermes

Fig. 29.8. House mark of Peter Vischer, a double sign of Hermes

Fig. 29.9. East Anglian house marks

Fig. 29.10. Printer's mark of George and Enguilbert de Marnef, with house mark, ca. 1500. The Library of the European Tradition.

When printing was invented, printers soon developed their own printers' devices to identify themselves. Some used traditional house marks, such as that in Enguilbert and George de Marnef's device of 1481 shown in figure 29.10, which has the family mark, accompanied by a symbolic engraving of the pelican in her piety, an emblem of personal sacrifice for the good of others.

Herman Boengart's 1472 glyph has a panoply of glyphs: a heart, six-pointed stars, fleur-de-lys, sun and moon, wild man and woman, and monograms of Jesus and Mary as well as personal initials and house marks (fig. 29.11). The mark of John de Colonia and Nicolas Jenson (from 1481) had a device that anticipates modern logos, though it is based on traditional symbology (fig. 29.12).

Fig. 29.11. Printer's mark of Herman Boengart, late 1400s. The Library of the European Tradition.

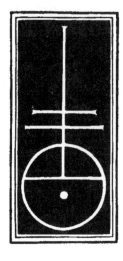

Fig. 29.12. Printer's mark of John de Colonia and Nicolas Jenson, Venice, 1481. The Library of the European Tradition.

The United Kingdom is a monarchy, so everything in the kingdom is ultimately the property of the sovereign. Even freehold property is technically the crown's, the current freeholder having only the right to sell the current freehold to anyone else. Swans, like the royal fishes (whales and sturgeons), are the direct property of the crown, marked on the bill in the ceremony of swan upping. In the East Anglian fen lands, there were four royal swan marks allocated by the swanmote at Wisbech. The swan mark sigils are varied in form, though many are clearly in the same current as merchants' and masons' marks. A few appear runic in inspiration, while others are simplified heraldry (Ticehurst 1937, 129). Girling observed that linear marks are similar to runes or combinations of runes (Girling 1964, 104). The question of whether we call a rune a letter of one of the recognized ancient futharks* or if we use the wider meaning determines our point of view; we must also consider what symbolic or magical meaning the user ascribes to it. The magical glyph known as the Ipswich warding sign is also known as a house mark (Pennick 2004, 146–47). The relationship between glyphs is always mutable, and there is no definitive answer. A few marks are actual monograms made from the initials of the owner.

These traditional marks continue to evolve. In the latter part of the nineteenth century, a renewed interest in traditional craftsman-

---

*Futhark is the name given to the runic "alphabet," as the letters start in the order f, u, th, a, r, k . . . not a, b, c.

ship led to a renaissance of the handicrafts. Craftsmen devised new marks, sometimes based on traditional European sigils and sometimes on the Japanese seals visible on the woodblock prints fashionable at the end of the nineteenth century. Die Wiener Werkstätte (the Viennese Workshops), operated from 1903 until 1932. The workshops' trademark, monogram, and the personal marks of its two leading designers, Josef Hoffmann and Koloman Moser, are shown in figure 29.13.

Fig. 29.13. Publicity for the Die Wiener Werkstätte, 1905, showing trademark, WW monogram, and monograms of the two leading designers. The Library of the European Tradition.

Fig. 29.14. Craftsmen's monograms,
Die Wiener Werkstätte.
The Library of the European Tradition.

The individual craft workers of the guild each had their own marks. A few are shown in figure 29.14. Toward the end of Die Wiener Werkstätte, the form of many of its marks was adopted as the monogrammic logo of the Volkswagen automobile company (fig. 29.15).

Fig. 29.15. *VW* glyph of the Volkswagen automobile company

Monograms are another current of glyph making, combining letters of a name or initials to make a sigil. They were popular in late antiquity, standing for the names of gods, demons, and human beings. The combination of the Greek letters *chi* and *rho* as the monogram of Christ has been mentioned in the "Crosses" section, on page 55. Emperors both in the Byzantine Empire at Constantinople and the Holy Roman Empire were signed by monograms, as were bishops and even cities. (Pennick 1991b, 69; 1996b, 88–92). Anglo-Saxon coins minted at London have the London monogram.

During the same period, rune masters were conjoining runes to create bind runes of power. The medieval black-letter alphabet lends itself to the creation of decorative monograms. The *IHS* glyph of Jesus (*Iesus Hominem Salvator,* meaning "Jesus Savior of Men") and the sign of Mary are shown in figures 29.16 and 29.17. These monograms appear ornamentally in church furnishings and sometimes in stone, as in the crowned monogram of Mary on the exterior of the Roman Catholic shrine at Walsingham, Norfolk, shown in figure 29.18.

Fig. 29.16. Gothic black-letter *IHS* monogram

Fig. 29.17. Mary monogram

Fig. 29.18. Twentieth-century Mary monogram in stone on the outer wall of a building at the Roman Catholic National Shrine of Our Lady at Walsingham, Norfolk

30. MISCELLANEOUS MAGICAL GLYPHS

Talismans and empowered glyphs are a magical means of warding off harm and bringing good fortune. Northern Europe has a complete range of these glyphs emerging from several cultural currents, but constructed according to the same magical principles. The *aegishjalmur* (helm of awe), otherwise *eagershelm,* is a northern tradition sigil to bring irresistible power. An eight-branched glyph with twenty-four crosspieces, it evokes wholeness in the form of the eight directions, the eight tides of the day, and the twenty-four hours.

It appears as the *escarbuncle* in heraldry and on Scottish Highland metalwork. The example illustrated in figure 30.1 is one of my paintings. Well known in Icelandic magic, the helm of awe is just one of a series of glyphs, some of them runic that are employed by magicians to bring about desired results (Davídsson 1903, 150–67; Flowers 1989, 71–102). The *lásabrjótur* (lock breaker, otherwise known as castle breaker), used to open locked doors magically and thereby to gain entry, is shown in figure 30.2. Insigils are glyphs composed of a number of characters or signs enclosed in a circle or square.

Fig. 30.1. The *aegishjalmur* (helm of awe), otherwise *eagershelm*, sigil of irresistible power used in Icelandic and Scottish magical traditions, and known as the *escarbuncle* in Anglo-French heraldry. Painting by the author.

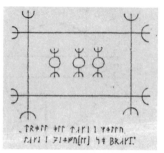

Fig. 30.2. Icelandic *lásabrjótur* (lock breaker, otherwise known as castle breaker) magical sigil, collected by Óláfur Davídsson, 1903. The Library of the European Tradition.

Feisifín (Fionn's shield) is an ancient Irish glyph associated with the hero Fionn Mac Cumhaill (Finn McCool). There are two forms, square and round, both illustrated in figures 30.3 and 30.4. Another name for the round one is Fionn's wheel. All of the letters of the Ogham script are written around it, a form of denoting comprehensiveness and completeness, as does the helm of awe. Figure 30.5 shows another form of the Ogham insigil. The nameless art of East Anglia likewise has a number of glyphs that appear unique to the tradition (fig. 30.6).

The four-cornered knot is the glyph signifying aspects of the

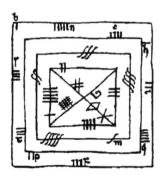

Fig. 30.3. Fionn's shield, (square) from *The Book of Ballymote*. The Library of the European Tradition.

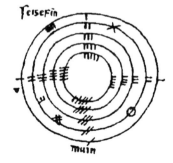

Fig. 30.4. Fionn's wheel, from *The Book of Ballymote*. The Library of the European Tradition.

Fig. 30.5. Irish Ogham insigil

Fig. 30.6. Sigil of the nameless art
of East Anglia.

Fig. 30.7. Old Scratch's gate, East
Anglian glyph to ward off harmful
influences on doorways, passages,
and crossing points. Stained-glass
light-catcher designed and made by
the author, 2004.

tradition itself. A blocking glyph, Old Scratch's gate, in the form of a stained-glass panel that I made, is shown in figure 30.7. This glyph serves to block sprite-infested passages and doors (Pennick 1995b, 117). The standard East Anglian glyph for banishing harmful things, as seen scribed on old bricks, is the X-with-dots, and another is the Ipswich warding sign, mentioned in the "House Marks, Craftsmen's Marks, and Sigils" section (page 166) as a house mark, but here used as a rune of protection. There are equivalent talismanic glyphs in all other currents of the European tradition; their sheer number and multiplicity have never been studied comprehensively, because any individual must concentrate on his or her own tradition to be able to use it effectively. In Great Britain alone are dozens of traditions, ranging through the *lijahs* of the Black Country to the wizards of the Scottish Highlands, the maritime magic of Scarborough and Whitby, the wise men and women of Wales, London occultism, the nameless art, and the industrial magic of Sheffield and Manchester. And there are more: every country and region in Europe has its own particular versions.

31. ALTERNATIVE AND NEW SPIRITUAL GLYPHS

Fig. 31.1. A selection of alchemical sigils all standing for the same substance— quicksilver (mercury). From the *Meicinisch-Chymisch und Alcemistisches Oraculum* (1783). The Library of the European Tradition.

We live in a literalistic age, and even many ancient faiths insist that sigils and glyphs have fixed meanings that can never develop further. But we have seen how early Christians used the swastika and variants of the ankh to denote their religious affiliation. But all glyphs not derived directly from a perceived phenomenon like the disc of the sun, or from the basics of geometry, like the triangle, pentagram, hexflower, and hexagram, are a matter of agreement and convention. The sigils shown in figure 31.1 are from the *Medicinisch-chymisch-und alchemistisches Oraculum,* published at Ulm, Germany, in 1783.*

---

*Full title: *Medicinisch-chymisch-und alchemistisches Oraculum, darinnen man nicht nur alle Zeichen und Abkürzungen, welche so wohl in den Recepten und Büchern der Aerzte und Apothecker als auch in den Schriften der Chemisten und Alchemisten vorkommen.* Ulm: Rosten der Stettinischen, 1783.

All thirty-nine of these glyphs were used at the time to denote the same thing: the metal mercury, otherwise called quicksilver, *Argentium vivum*, or *Hydragyrum*. The elegance of these glyphs is intrinsically attractive, one of a metal and one of an alloy: platinum and bronze.

The customary glyphs of divinatory geomancy are another case of flexibility and development. Primarily a system of divination based on binary mathematics, divinatory geomancy acquired an astronomical connection as the correspondence of the sixteen figures to the world was worked out (Skinner 1980, 120–47). In his *Fourth Book of Occult Philosophy*, Heinrich Cornelius Agrippa depicted the sixteen geomantic figures as groups of stars and related them to planetary powers. The diagram in figure 31.2 shows Agrippa's starry figures and figure 31.3 shows the relationship of two of Agrippa's star figures to more developed glyphs used to denote the geomantic figures (Pennick 1995c, 69, 114).

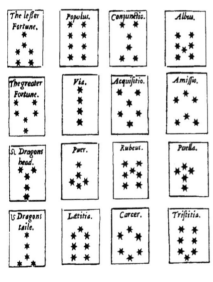

Fig. 31.2. Glyphs or geomantic figures in divinatory geomancy

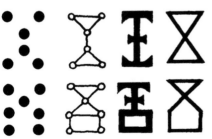

Fig. 31.3. Corresponding forms of two of Agrippa's star figures with glyphs from divinatory geomancy. Top row: *Conjunctio*. Bottom Row: *Rubeus*. Drawing by the author.

Glyphs used in a spiritual context are open to development. They are not fixed bygones, preserved as a spectacle for people roaming the tourist trail of history. The radical tradition develops the new from within the currents of tradition; it does not break the continuity, but reinvigorates it in new ways appropriate to contemporary developments. One means is by the assemblage of glyphs in the manner of the bind rune and the monogram.

In 1564 John Dee published his famous new glyph, the hieroglyphic monad, shown in figure 31.4. In his book *Oedipus Aegyptiacus*, published in Rome in 1653, Athanasius Kircher analyzed Dee's monad as a combination of planetary powers, as shown in figure 31.5.

Fig. 31.4. The hieroglyphic monad devised by John Dee in 1564

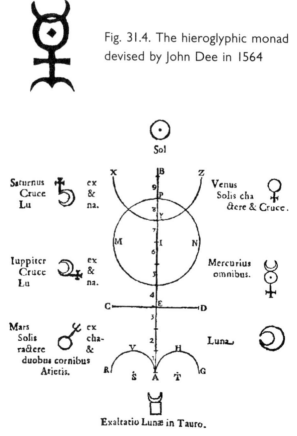

Fig. 31.5. Glyphic analysis by Athanasius Kircher in *Oedipus Aegyptiacus* (1653) of John Dee's hieroglyphic monad. The Library of the European Tradition.

Another sigil, shown in figure 31.6, is from 1967, devised by Frederick Adams for the Californian pagan community Feraferia. It is a tree-of-life glyph called the Phytalia, whose lower part symbolizes the roots in winter, its main stem the trunk of the tree, and the first cross-piece the leaves of autumn; the oval part is the summer fruit and the sun, and the upper the flowering branches, the crown, horns, and star (Adams 1967, 7).

Fig. 31.6. The Feraferia glyph with explanation of
its meanings by Frederick Adams, 1967.
The Library of the European Tradition.

Both Dee and Adams, more than five centuries apart, are examples of people with symbolic knowledge who extended our repertoire of symbolic glyphs. The possibilities have still not come to an end, even in the materialist and literalist twenty-first century.

32. LOCAL GLYPHS

Context is everything, and local history and tradition maintain certain ways of doing things that have to be explained to visitors, if indeed the locals know that they are unusual in any way. Local magical sigils are, of course, part of this, but they occur in secular contexts that reflect local identity in particular, often unique, ways. This happens in all vernacular traditions, even in the way that public services are provided. Although route numbers are used on most buses, subways, and trams today, glyphs, emblems, and colored signs are an alternative, immediately recognizable to passengers standing at bus, subway, or tram stops. In the early twentieth century, the Dublin United Tramways Company, the first electric tramway (streetcar) system in that city, distinguished routes by colored metal glyphs mounted on top of the destination box on each end of the tram car. Thus, for example, trams running between Rathfarnham and Whitehall bore a green Maltese cross; those on the Inchicore to Westland Row service, a brown oval. The College Green to Drumcondra route was marked by an inverted white ace of spades, Terenure to Rathmines a red triangle, the Dalkey line a green shamrock, and Glasnevin to Rialto a brown lozenge (Corcoran 2000, 62–63). In other contexts these colored shapes are given other meanings. Route numbers are sometimes shown in different colors or on different-colored destination blinds, as on the Antwerp tramways, where the route 4 number and destination is displayed in black lettering on a blue blind, route 7 is in white on black, 10 is in black on green, 11 in red lettering on a white background, and 12 lettered in white on a red background.

Color-coding of tram routes in Amsterdam in parallel with numbers is the local practice, originating in 1904. The destination blinds' colored squares are in various two-color combinations of different colors: green, yellow, red, white, and blue, except route 3, which is a yellow square; route 9, which is a green square; route 10 a red one; and route 22 a pink square. The single-color-square routes were originally the tangential lines, while the others marked the radial routes. Blue-green and white-yellow combinations have never been used. In 1948 it was proposed to abolish the route colors in Amsterdam, but there was a public outcry and they remained. New colors were allocated in 1989 up to route number 30, some for routes that did not yet exist, and new express routes 50 and 58 were allocated colors then, along with others numbered in the 50s and not yet used. The tram routes in Sheffield that date from the inauguration of the present system in 1994 have colored squares and no numbers. As in Amsterdam only the trams in Sheffield carry colors, not the buses, which are numbered (fig. 32.1).

Fig. 32.1. Tram destination glyphs. *Top left:* Brussels, Belgium, 1968, route number in black on white circular board; *top right:* Amsterdam, the Netherlands, 1968, route number 16 in white on black with two-color indicator square, blue (top) and yellow; *bottom left:* Antwerp, Belgium, 2004, number 10 and destination in black on green; *bottom right:* Sheffield, England, 2003, destination in white on black, yellow route indication square.

33. SYMBOLIC BEASTS

Some animals have taken on the mantle of symbolic forms, appearing not only in human mythology but also as figurative symbols of particular qualities. Here I will deal with a few of the many beasts that have found their way into symbolism. There are several categories of symbolic beasts. First, those that exist as they are: like the lion, emblem of courage, fortitude, and strength. Then those that exist and have symbolic tales attached to them, such as the pelican that bites its breast so that its chicks can feed on its blood. This is a Christian symbol of self-sacrifice, shown in a nineteenth-century engraving of a medieval stained-glass window in Notre-Dame Cathedral, Paris (fig. 33.1).

Fig. 33.1. Drawing by Emile Leconte, 1843, of a medieval stained-glass window in Notre-Dame Cathedral, Paris, showing the pelican in her piety. The Library of the European Tradition.

There also are those beasts that once existed, such as the European wild bull called the auroch, from which the second rune *ur* is named, which is no longer in existence, having been hunted to extinction: the last one was shot in Poland in 1627. There also are those beasts that appear close by as an ostentum, like the miraculous stag with a cross of light between its antlers encountered by St. Hubertus (fig. 33.2), or various beasts, such as stags, pigs, and bears, implicated in the foundation of churches (Pennick 1996a, 168–72; Pennick and Field 2004, 138–45).

Fig. 33.2. The stag seen by St. Hubertus (a.k.a. Hubert, Humbert, and Humber), with the cross of light between its antlers. The Library of the European Tradition.

Fig. 33.3. Pargeted stag in wreath, Dunmow, Essex

The appearances of black dogs, water beasts, and dragons comes into this category (comprehensive details of dragons and dragon lore can be found in my 1997 book *Dragons of the West* [1997c]). Then there are those animals that were formerly said to exist somewhere in far-off lands, named by writers of the miraculous, the weird, the wonderful, and the absurd, from Pliny to Rabelais. We read of sphinx and cockatrice, manticore and basilisk; scolopendres, penphredons, scalavotins, and cuhersks; illicines, nightmares, alhatrabans, salamanders, megalaunes, and suckling water snakes. Among them are numbered the phoenix and the Scythian tarand, an animal wonderful for its ability to

Fig. 33.4. Stone unicorn,
College of Heralds, London

alter the color of its skin and fur according to the colors of neighboring things. This category also includes the yale and the unicorn, both important emblems in heraldry. A unicorn guarding the College of Heralds in London is shown in figure 33.4.

Apart from the pelican and the dragon, the serpent, the phoenix, the cockerel, and the peacock have a large body of symbolic lore attached to them. The following four sections are about them.

34. THE SERPENT

Fig. 34.1. The crowned serpent glyph

A snake in the shape of a ring, with its tail in its mouth, is symbolic of time, eternity, the unity of matter, and the circularity of the alchemical process. The illustration of Saturn (fig. 34.2) is from Andrew Tooke's *The Pantheon,* published in 1764, showing him with the traditional attributes of time—the encircled serpent and the scythe that cuts off existence. As the Worm Ouroboros, the circling serpent is a symbol mentioned in *The Poem of the Philosopher Theophrastus upon the Sacred Art,* an eighth- or ninth-century anonymous text on alchemy (Linden 2003, 65–66). The poet describes Ouroboros as a dragon that devours

Fig. 34.2. The god Kronos-Saturn with his attributes: the Worm Ouroboros and the scythe. Eighteenth-century engraving. The Library of the European Tradition.

his tail until nothing remains, a savior who, by his help, all Earth-born are sustained abundantly in life. This eighteenth-century engraving of Saturn shows him holding up Ouroboros as an emblem of time. The Midgardsorm, the world serpent called Iormungand, encircles the globe at the bottom of the ocean in Norse mythology. The struggle of Thor against it is the theme of "Hymiskviðr," where the thunder god goes fishing, catches the *orm,* and threatens to pull it from the seabed. Then his companion, the giant Hymir, cuts the hawser lest the death of the serpent bring on the end of the world. The parallel lines between which it was customary to write runes were frequently made to represent a serpent. In the nineteenth century, the Theosophical Society, seeking universal symbols, amalgamated Ouroboros with the swastika, the hexagram, and the ankh to make their sigil (fig. 34.3).

Fig. 34.3. Late nineteenth-century badge of the Theosophical Society with the Worm Ouroboros allied to various other glyphs including the ankh, the swastika, and the hexagram. The Library of the European Tradition.

Fig. 34.4. Cartouche with the caduceus of Mercury,
Esslingen-am-Neckar, Germany

The winged staff with two serpents snaking around it is the caduceus, the rod of Hermes, god of information and trade, called Mercury by the Romans, as shown in an architectural setting in figure 34.4. A rod with a single serpent is the staff of Asklepios, Greek god of healing, the Roman Aesculapius. Christian iconography adopted the serpent and staff of Asklepios in images of the Adam and Eve myth where the Tree of Knowledge has the serpent of temptation twined around it.

Fig. 34.5. Runestone at Ståång, Södermanland, Sweden, with an older central runic inscription and surrounding serpentine band of later runes with union knot. The Library of the European Tradition.

In an age where glyphs are used inappropriately, we may see the double-serpent rod of Hermes used ignorantly by medical authorities in error for the rod of Asklepios. During the twentieth century, the Asklepian rod transmogrified as an ambulance glyph, perhaps by way of the caduceus, into a version of the six-branched Chrismon, also known as the Old English *iar* rune, the *ior* rune of Northumbria, and the *hagal* of the Germanic rune masters. The latter rune is viewed as a stave of healing, and the *iar* and *ior* signify an aquatic beast, often identified as Iormungand, the world serpent.

During an epidemic of the plague in Rome in the Roman Year 461 (292 BCE), the augurs consulted the *Sybilline Books* about what to do about it and were told to bring Aesculapius to Rome from Epidauros. A ship was dispatched and the sacred serpent that was the embodiment of the god was brought to Rome. When the ship reached Rome, the serpent slipped overboard and swam to the island in the River Tiber. Here the shrine of medical healing was established (Matthäus 1987, 33–34). The Tiber Island was fashioned into a stone ship with the image of Aesculapius and his serpented staff near to the prow. A photograph of the image is shown in figure 34.6, but the face of the god was chiseled off in Christian times, and only the serpent and staff remain. The

Fig. 34.6. The staff of Aesculapius with his serpent remains to this day near the prow of the stone ship that the Tiber Island was converted into in 293 BCE. Religious zealots smashed the face off the god.

holy island had several temples, the principal of which was the Temple of Aesculapius, on which later churches dedicated to St. Bartholomew were raised. The island was a place of healing, and remains so today, with a hospital on the site of another temple.

Fig. 34.7. Veneration of a serpent in sixteenth-century Lithuania. From Olaus Magnus. The Library of the European Tradition.

The serpent and the pothook glyph are linked by their form. Until industrialized modernization made their lives intolerable, house snakes were kept in parts of central Europe, where they were viewed as the living soul of the house. Known as the *žaltys* sacred serpents were venerated in medieval Lithuania, as in the woodcut from the works of Olaus Magnus shown in figure 34.7 (Trinkūnas 1999, 214). A wrought-iron hanger for pothooks, suspended above the house fire, was sometimes made in serpentine form. A *Lauenburger Herdschlange* from Mölln near Ratzeburg, Germany, the seat of the goddess Siwa, is shown in figure 34.8. This example intertwined the tails in the form of a heart.

Fig. 34.8. Serpentine fire crane for hanging pots and kettles via pothooks over the fire. A *Lauenburger Herdschlange* from Mölln near Ratzeburg, Germany. The Library of the European Tradition.

35. THE PHOENIX

Fig. 35.1. The phoenix on a building in Exeter, Devon, in 1957, commemorating the reconstruction of the city center after its destruction by enemy action in World War II.

Perhaps the most potent symbol of all after the Great Fire is the phoenix, the prime symbol of continuity in renewal. It is, as Tickell writes, "A god-like Bird! Whose endless Round of Years, Out-lasts the Stars, and tires the circling Spheres" (Tickell 1751, vol. 2, 233). This mythic bird lives a thousand years, and then, in its decline, makes a funeral pyre of rare Sabaean herbs, in whose flames, kindled by the sun, the phoenix is cremated. From its own ashes the bird rises again, renewed in full vigor. In 1666, after the Great Fire, John Evelyn used the image of the city of London rising again like the phoenix (Evelyn 1894, vol. 3, 88). The phoenix is transcendent of time, but it is not immortal, for it dies repeatedly and undergoes eternal renewal. Thomas Tickell's poem "A Description of the Phoenix: From Claudia" celebrates this image of transcendent life:

> *Thrice happy Phoenix! Heav'n's peculiar Care*
> *Has made thyself thyself's surviving Heir;*
> *By death thy deathless Vigor is supply'd,*
> *Which sinks to Ruin all the World beside;*
> *Thy Age, not thee, assisting Phoebus burns,*
> *And vital Flames light up thy fun'ral Urns. . . .*
> *When Nature ceases, thou shalt still remain,*
> *Nor second Chaos bound thy endless Reign;*
> *Fate's tyrant Laws thy happier Lot shall brave,*
> *Baffle Destruction, and elude the Grave.*
> *(TICKELL 1751, 236–37)*

Fig. 35.2. Phoenix and sunburst sculpture by Caius Gabriel
Cibber, carved in the pediment of the south transept of St. Paul's
Cathedral, London, with the motto "Resurgam" (I shall rise again).
Drawing by the author, 2005.

The gable end of the south transept of St. Paul's Cathedral in
London has an arched center that continues the lines of the cherub-
headed window below. It is filled with a sculpture by Caius Gabriel
Cibber of the phoenix rising anew from its fiery pyre, its resplendent
rays radiating forth. The pyre burns on a plinth with the inscription
"Resurgam" (I shall rise again) (fig. 35.2). This memorialized an event
recounted in *Parentalia, or, Memoirs of the Family of the Wrens* (1750)
(the writings of Sir Christopher Wren's son, published by Sir C's grand-
son) that occurred in the ruins of Old St. Paul's when Sir Christopher
Wren was locating the place where the center of the dome—the omphalos of the new cathedral—would be (Wren 1750, 292). A laborer was
ordered to go to a nearby pile of rubble and bring back a flat stone
("such as should first come to Hand") to mark the central point. He
brought back a fragment of gravestone. On it was the single word in
large capitals: "Resurgam." It is clear that this was viewed as a symbolic
ostentum of providence.

The phoenix who rises again has a special relationship to the sun
god Phoebus, who provides the spark that lights the pyre. So it is appropriate that at St. Paul's the carving faces the south, the direction of the
sun at its midday height and the direction ascribed to fire in Hermetic
diagrams of the four quarters.

36. THE COCKEREL
AND WEATHERCOCKS

Christian writers noted the symbolism of the cock in their mythology. Although a symbol of watchfulness, the biblical story of Peter denying Jesus three times before cockcrow gives the cock connotations of unreliability. Geoffrey Chaucer likened the inconsistency he believed women to have with the "weathercock, that turneth his face with every wind," a contrary interpretation of the runic meaning of *wyn*, the vane, which always remains centered and in balance with the prevailing conditions. Weather vanes are very ancient, dating from the second millennium BCE or earlier, but the origin of cock-shaped ones—and other beast-shaped ones—is less certain. The Roman mausoleum of the Flavii at Cillium in North Africa had a weathercock with moving wings set atop the monument. In Athens in the first century BCE, a bronze triton served as the pointer of wind direction on the Tower of the Winds, designed by the Macedonian architect Andronicus of Cyrrhus (Pennick 2005b, 71).

The history of the weathercock between the days of Roman paganism and early medieval Christiandom is uncertain. Sometime after the year 500 CE, the Roman weathercock was adopted by Christian church builders. In England it appears as the solution to an eighth-century Anglo-Saxon riddle, and from Italy, France, Germany, and Switzerland, there are a number of records before the year 1000 CE. In the year 820 CE at Brescia, Italy, Bishop Rampertus set a metal weathercock on top of the tower of the church dedicated to St. Faustino Maggiore. This cock was found in 1652, with the fact recorded on it in a Latin inscription (Novati 1905, 497). The tradition of engraving the year the cock was made on it continues to this day. In his *Life of St. Swithin*, Wulfstan, an English monk who died in 990 CE, wrote how the bishop of Winchester had ordered a gilded weathercock to be set on top of his cathedral. Another monkish chronicler, Ekkehard of St. Gallen, Switzerland (ca. 980–1060 CE), records that in 925 CE, during the Hungarian invasion of Western Europe, they stole the weathercocks from churches in Bavaria to honor the *Deus Loci* (Ekkehard, *Casus St. Galli*, 82). Another record from the same era shows that after the defeat of the Hungarians, weathercocks were again erected, for in 965 CE, the weathercock on the abbey at Chalon-sur-Sâone, France, was blown down by lightning (Martin 1903–1904, 6). After 1000 CE references and records proliferate, often recording the erection of a weathercock on a new building or the replacement of an old one that had been struck by lightning. The eleventh-century Bayeux Tapestry shows a weathercock being set up on the new Westminster Abbey, and a drawing in the *Pontifical* of Rouen, France, from the same time, shows a weathercock on a church tower. In 1091 an English weathercock smith went to Coutances in Normandy at the request of Bishop Gaufroy de Montbray to make a new cock to replace one that had been destroyed by lightning. In 1219 lightning smashed the weathercock on the tower at the Abbey of St. Denis in Paris, and there are many other such records. The oldest English weathercock is the Whistling Cock at Ottery St. Mary in Devon. The Whistling Cock is hollow, made of cast bronze, with a brass comb (Mockridge and Mockridge 1990, 35, 57). Its name comes from its whistle tubes—tuned to the notes B and G—that sound when the wind reaches a certain speed. It was vandalized in recent years by the church authorities to reduce the sound after repeated complaints from those living near the church. These sound tubes resemble the *makelaar* on Dutch windmills that indicates wind speed to the miller by the sound it makes. Not only do whistling weathercocks indicate the wind's direction, but also its strength. Although the Whistling Cock at Ottery St. Mary now appears to be unique in Britain, there is a reference to another whistling cock that once existed on another St. Mary's church, at Exeter, ten miles away. An old chronicle, now in the Devon Record Office, records that in October 1501, Katherine of Aragon was staying at the dean's house in the cathedral close. The weather was very windy, making the weathercock on the nearby church of St. Mary Major whistle so loudly that the princess could not sleep. So a man was ordered to climb the tower in a storm in the middle of the night to take it down, which he did. "After her departure," the chronicle tells us, "the same was put up again" (Orme 1986, 53). A medieval Devon cock is shown in figure 36.1 on its eight-sided tower at Colyton, Devon.

Fig. 36.1. Weathercock in situ atop the octagonal tower (the eight winds) of the church at Colyton, Devon

Although some ancient cocks are hollow, such as the 1428 cock on Sheffield Anglican Cathedral, most are made from flat sheet metal and covered with gold leaf that reflects the sunlight. The retired weathercock shown in figure 36.2, from Neuss in Germany, was fashioned by a blacksmith from sheet metal. Also, because they are constantly subject

Fig. 36.2. Retired medieval weathercock of copper, Neuss, Germany

to the weather, it is rare for a weathercock to last six hundred years. Periodic regilding helps to preserve them, and they can last a long time. It is recorded that the cock of Old St. Paul's in London was regilded on five separate occasions before it and the spire, at the time the tallest building in the world—one hundred feet taller than the Great Pyramid—were blown down in 1505. The tradition of weathercocks still goes on. The weathercock that topped the Runestaff Crafts workshop, which I made in 1984 and is shown in figure 36.3, lasted only a few years before it was blown down in a gale and destroyed. The workshop itself was blown down in a later storm (Pennick 2006d, 107–8). A later weathercock design, as yet unmade, is illustrated in figure 36.4.

Fig. 36.3. Weathercock on the Runestaff Crafts workshop, 1985, made by the author. Destroyed.

Fig. 36.4. Weathercock. Drawing by the author, 2002.

Cocks are the most common traditional church weather vanes, but other animals—real and legendary—are used. It seems that dragons were never set up as vanes on Roman Catholic churches, but after the Reformation they were acceptable to English Protestants. A sixteenth-century weatherdragon, the oldest in England, is at Newark Park, Ozleworth, Gloucestershire. The most notable dragon vane in England surmounts the steeple of St. Mary-le-Bow in London. Designed by Sir Christopher Wren, the church replaced an earlier one burned in the Great Fire of London in 1666. Made by coppersmith Robert Bird, it measures eight feet in length (Pennick 2005b, 129–31). Wren used the dragon because it is one of the emblems of London, being a bearer of the coat of arms of the city. The London dragon is depicted with a red cross beneath each wing. South of the river in London, the church of St. James in Bermondsey has a dragon cast from bronze that was once part of Napoléon's cannon, captured at the Battle of Waterloo and subsequently melted down to make bells and weather vanes for English churches.

The European tradition tells that there are eight primary winds, related to the eight tides of the day in the northern tradition. An Icelandic magical diagram for finding the way has the sigils of the eight winds on an eight-rayed sigil (fig. 36.5). Of course, the winds' names and characters vary from place to place, as befitting place-specific qualities (Pennick 1999a, 145–61). Figure 36.6 shows the classical Mediterranean names of the winds along with correspondences with the times of day, the four elements, the four seasons, and the four humors.

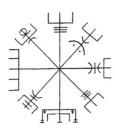

Fig. 36.5. Waymarker magical sigil collected by Ólafur Davídsson, 1903, with glyphs of the eight directions or winds. The Library of the European Tradition.

All such virtues and qualities of existence have their corresponding place in what we call the scheme of things. The traditional view of the winds is that they are of a spirit nature. In the folklore of the Alps, the spirits called *Heiden* (pagans) are said to control or affect the weather.

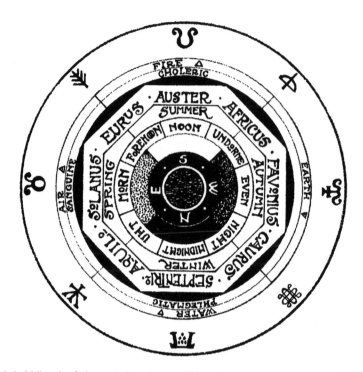

Fig. 36.6. Wheel of the winds, times of day, elements, seasons, and humors. Drawing by the author.

When the sun shines in the rain, "the Heiden are having a wedding" (Vernaliken 1858, 421). In the Oberpfalz in Germany the wind is personified as a giant, the "Christian-Eater" (Bächtold-Stäubli, 1927–1942, vol. 3, 1648). There is a German magical practice of feeding the wind with corn, seeds, bread, and salt put on the windowsill (Bächtold-Stäubli, 1927–1942, vol. 4, 643). The winds are traditionally shown as blowing faces, as depicted in the central European wind god Püsterich (Franz 1943, 62–76, plate XII) and in the glyph from a sixteenth-century portable sundial made in Nuremberg, Germany (fig. 36.7).

Fig. 36.7. Wind glyph from a sixteenth-century ivory sundial, Nuremberg, Germany

37. THE EYE AND
THE PEACOCK

The single-eye glyph, usually of a right human eye, is called variously the eye of Horus, the eye of providence, the all-seeing eye, the radiant eye, and the eye of omnipresence. As a Masonic emblem it is said not to be derived from the Egyptian glyph, which signified divine royal power, but to be derived from Christian contexts, where it is a symbol of God (Cooper 2006, 116). It is a literal rendition of the knot called Godsoog, appearing on Dutch fishermen's knitwear and as a barroom glyph in Low Countries fishing ports with the warning admonition, "God sees you" (Van der Klift-Tellegen 1987, 19, 34–35). Eyelike patterns appear in nature as a warning, as on the peacock and the butterfly named after it. A displaying peacock is a striking sight, its eye patterns making a deep impression on us (fig. 37.1). The peacock is the bird attribute of the goddess Juno, and hence emblematic of her protection as an alternative to the hexflower glyph, also emblematic of the goddess.

All-seeing eyes appear in profusion in peacocky style in Renaissance paintings of the wings of both archangels and dragons. But the peacock

Fig. 37.1. A displaying peacock

Fig. 37.2. Eye-mark pargeting on a house in Dunmow, Essex, using bottlenecks to make the pattern, nineteenth century

is also an image of one of the seven deadly sins of Christian doctrine, the sin of pride. As a glyph the eye or the many eyes of the peacock is a pattern intended to ward off harm, as in the old peacock wall made in pargeting work from Dunmow, Essex, using the necks of bottles (fig. 37.2).

Fig. 37.3. A Bunzlau teapot and plate, with hand-painted *Pfauenaugen* decoration

The *Pfauenaugen* pattern, as in the Bunzlau (Boleslawiek) pottery painting style of Poland and Germany, is shown on a teapot and plate in figure 37.3. But the peacock feather itself is superstitiously shunned in the British folk tradition, which tells that it is unlucky to have one in a house and that young women cannot expect ever to be married if peacock feathers are kept as ornaments (*Notes & Queries*, 8th series, IV [1893], 531). I have had shocked reactions from visitors who suddenly noticed a peacock feather sticking out of one of my art nouveau vases. The carved slate mantelpiece in a house in Snowdonia, Wales, shown in figure 37.4, has a roundel pattern that may represent the eyes of the peacock or have some other meaning, too.

Fig. 37.4. Carved slate eighteenth-century mantelpiece over the fireplace of a farmhouse in Snowdonia, Wales, showing eyelike roundels and seemingly significant numbers

38. THE SIGILS OF MAMMON

Of all human institutions, money is perhaps the invention most separated from the natural world, one inextricably tied up with power over the materials of the world and other humans. The legends of Midas and the more modern misers tell of the waning of humaneness in those to whom the accumulation of money has become the sole objective of living, with money giving them the power to accumulate further wealth. For money has become the measure of all human activity. Every human capacity and material object is measured in terms of money. This is more than mere numerology, that superstitious worship of numbers where they are revered in their own right as a means to gain and retain power. "Lies, damned lies, and statistics" is the old expression, meaning that statistics, like other measurements of the real world by artificial parameters, has become not only an observation on reality, but also is considered more real than the reality it purports to describe. The sigils of money, including the pound, dollar, and euro, stand for the means

Fig. 38.1. Two of the sigils of Mammon, the British pound sterling and the United States dollar

of life and death (fig. 38.1). The pound sigil is derived from the letter *L,* standing for *Libra,* the pound weight of the Roman Empire. The United States dollar has a confused identity. Its name is a version of the central European Valley silver coin, the thaler, but its sign is derived from the figure *8,* for the Spanish *real de a ocho* coins, known as "pieces of eight." The euro, as a late twentieth-century invention, has a stylized letter *E.* These historically derived signs are as powerful as any magical sigil used to summon a demonic entity. The power to spend money is literally the power to remain alive, to have one's being in society. Those without money are the invisible ones, powerless and doomed to a miserable, precarious existence, if they survive at all. Those without money are in the condition that the old Welsh bards gave as one of the epithets of the underworld of Annwn, "the loveless place." Society is driven by the belief that if one has nothing, one *is* nothing. For the ancient Jewish sages personified the place where Abraham dwelt as a god of unrighteous power called Mammon. For one can never be loved for oneself in this realm of Mammon; one's value is judged by one's possessions, and one's possessions are measured by money. Along with other spiritual teachers, Jesus taught that one cannot serve both Mammon and God, that is, cannot worship material wealth and the world of the spiritual (Luke 16:13). Yet how many pulpit professionals of all religions today dress in the finest clothes, eat the costliest foods, and ride in limousines? That the glyph for money is a human abstraction, which has no intrinsic value, no value at all outside the narrow confines of human culture, is shown by the banknotes in figure 38.2.

Issued in Germany the five hundred mark note of 1922 was worthless by the time the two million mark note was issued in August 1923. This historical example is a warning to all political and philosophical theories that claim, knowingly or unconsciously, that money is the true reality of human existence.

Fig. 38.2. The relative values of these two German Reichsbank notes tell the story of the collapse of the German currency, the Reichsmark, between 1922 and 1923. Author's collection.

39. THE DEATH'S HEAD

Death is personified as the Grim Reaper, a skeleton with an hourglass and scythe, as in the eighteenth-century Dutch emblem, *"Myn glas loopt ras"* (my glass runs fast), shown in figure 39.1. The scythe is also an

Fig. 39.1. Seventeenth-century Dutch emblem of the inevitable passage of time leading to death: *"Myn glas loopt ras"* (my glass runs fast), with the race allegory of the tortoise arriving, slow but sure. The Library of the European Tradition.

FLYNS

Wie derfelbe in denen Annalibus Budissin beschrieben wird, u bey dē Dorff Oyne auf eint Kašengořad ha foll.

Fig. 39.2. Engraving of the central European god of death, Flyns, with emblems of fire and lion, irresistible forces of destruction. From *Lausitzische Merkwürdigkeiten* by S. Grosser, Leipzig, Germany, 1714. The Library of the European Tradition.

emblem of Saturn as the god of time, and it links with the shears of Atropos and Skuld that cut the thread of human life or shear the web of wyrd apart when we die. There are few specific gods of death in Europe, but in central Europe, images were made of Flyns. One is depicted in figure 39.2 with his attributes, the all-consuming images of fire and the lion, against which unaided humans cannot fight. The arrow of time, against which we have no defense, is another glyph of mortality.

Skulls, an emblem of mortality, were common in former years on graveyard memorials. The death's head was a common image on tombstones, sometimes paired with winged hourglasses, symbolizing the transience of life. On two of the eight sides of the Oostkerk in Middelburg in the Netherlands are macabre stone swags or garlands depicting human bones and winged hourglasses with one bird's and one bat's wing, showing that time flies continuously whether it is day or night (fig. 39.3).

The skull and crossbones is a common graveyard emblem on British tombstones from the seventeenth and eighteenth centuries. It bears a similarity to the Chi-Rho monogram of Christ. They are prevalent in the London classical churches built after the Great Fire of London in 1666, especially ones that were located in earlier burial grounds or had churchyards for burials provided when built new (Pennick 2005b). The graveyard at St. Nicholas, Deptford, had prominent skull carvings, and

Fig. 39.3. Sculpted stone garland composed of the bones of the human skeleton. On the hanging parts are hourglasses with two wings, each having one of a bird and one a bat, signifying that time flies whether it is day or night. The Oostkerk, Middelburg, Zeeland.

there were stone skulls impaled on iron spikes at St. Olave on Hart Street. At that time real human heads of executed rebels could be seen impaled on iron spikes on top of the city gates of London and York.

Until the early twentieth century, soldiers of the elite Prussian Army unit called the Death's Head Hussars wore black busbies, each of which sported a large metal skull on the front to show their enemies that they offered no quarter. One is shown in figure 39.4.

Fig. 39.4. Death's head badge from a busby of the elite Prussian Army unit called the Death's Head Hussars. Nineteenth century.

The black flag has long been a sign that the attackers in a fight will give no quarter, that is, take no prisoners, but kill everyone. It was adopted as an anarchist emblem in 1832 (Anon. 1983, 12), but it was used much earlier as a pirate flag as well as in military sieges where the besieged had refused to surrender. The black flag called the Jolly Roger is best known as the flag of pirates and buccaneers, bearing the skull-and-crossbones emblem (fig. 39.5).

Fig. 39.5. The Jolly Roger

In 1982 when the British Royal Navy's nuclear submarine *Conqueror* returned to port from the Falklands War, it flew the Jolly Roger to celebrate its sinking of the Argentinian Navy's capital ship, the cruiser *General Belgrano*. Such is the image of death and the devil that is binding the world in chains (fig. 39.6). Those philosophies that do not seek to bring more misery and premature death to the world attempt to provide some understanding of such a bleak view of human existence.

Fig. 39.6. Death and the devil cooperate in chaining the world. Baroque allegorical ceiling painting, St. Mang's Monastery, Füssen, Germany.

BIBLIOGRAPHY

Ab Ithel, J. Williams, trans. 1867. *Barddas; or, a Collection of Original Documents, Illustrative of the Theology, Wisdom, and Usages of The Bardo-Druidic System of the Isle of Britain.* 2 vols. Llandovery, Wales: The Welsh Manuscripts Society.

Adams, Frederick. 1967. "Principal Symbol: The Phytalia (Tree Power)." *Feraferia* 1: 7.

Agrell, Sigurd. 1927. *Runornas talmystik och dess antika förebild.* Lund, Sweden: Vetensabssocieteten I.

———. 1931. *Senantik mysteriereligion og Nordisk runmagi.* Stockholm: Bonniers.

———. 1934. *Lapptrummor och runmagi.* Lund, Sweden: Glerup.

Akhtar, Miriam, and Steve Humphries. 1999. *Far Out: The Dawning of New Age Britain.* Bristol: Sansom & Co.

Alberti, Leon Battista. 1755. *The Ten Books of Architecture* [De re aedificatoria]. Translated by Giacomo Leoni. London: Edward Owen.

Anati, Emmanuel. 1976. *Evolution and Style in Camunian Rock Art.* Translated by Larryn Diamond. Capo di Ponte, Italy: Edizioni del Centro.

Andersen, S. A. 1945. *Guldehornene fra Gallehus.* Copenhagen: Populært Videnskabeligt Forlag.

Anon. 1783. *Medicinisch-chymisch-und alchemistisches Oraculum, darinnen man nicht nur alle Zeichen und Abkürzungen, welche so wohl in den Recepten und Büchern der Aerzte und Apothecker als auch in den Schriften der Chemisten und Alchemisten vorkommen.* Ulm, Germany: Rosten der Stettinischen.

Anon. ca. 1860. *The Manual of Heraldry.* London: Arthur Hall, Virtue & Co.

Anon. 1983. "Graffitic Symbolism: The Anarchist 'A'". *The Symbol* 1: 12.

Amberlain, Robert. 1962. "Jean-Julien Champagne, Alias Fulcanelli: Dossier Fulcanelli." *Cahiers de la Tour Saint-Jacques* 9.

Appulm, Horset, ed. 1994. *Johann Siebmacher's Wappenbuch* (1605). Dortmund, Germany: Horst Appuhn.

Ashton, Chris. 1982. "Nigel Pennick Interview." *Quicksilver Messenger* 11: 3–12.

Aswynn, Freya. 1988. *Leaves of Yggdrasil*. London: Aswynn.

Ayres, James. 1977. *British Folk Art*. London: Barrie & Jenkins Ltd.

Bächtold-Stäubli, Hanns, ed. 1927–1942. *Handwörterbuch des Deutschen Aberglaubens*. 9 vols. Berlin: Koehler und Amerlang.

Balzli, Johannes. 1917. *Guido v. List. Der Wiederentdecker Uralter Arischer Weisheit. Sein Leben und sein Schaffen*. Vienna: Guido-von-List Gesellschaft.

Banks, M. M. 1935. "Tangled Thread Mazes." *Folk-Lore* 46: 78–80.

Baring-Gould, Sabine. 1901. *A Book of Brittany*. London: Methuen.

Barnes, Richard. 1983. *The Sun in the East: Norfolk and Suffolk Fairs*. Kirstead, England: RB Photographic.

Bärtsch, Albert. 1993. *Holz Masken: Fastnachts- und Maskenbrauchtum in der Schweiz, in Süddeutschland und Österreich*. Aarau, Switzerland: AT Verlag.

Bayley, J. "Non-ferrous Metalworking: Continuity and Change." In *Science and Archaeology: Glasgow 1987,* ed. E. Slater and J. O. Tate, 193–208. Oxford: British Archaeological Reports, British Series 196.

Beaumont, R. M. 1922. *The Builders of Southwell Minster and Their Marks*. Southwell, England: privately published.

Behrend, Michael, and Debbie Saward, trans. 1982. *Trojaburgen: The Works of Aspelin, Hamkens, Sieber, and Mössinger*. Thundersley and Bar Hill, England: The Caerdroia Project and the Institute of Geomantic Research.

Berchorius, Petrus. *Repertorium Morale*. Nuremberg: Anton Koberger, 1489/1499.

Berry, Jason. 2004. "Mardi Gras in New Orleans, USA: Annals of a Queen." In *Carnival!* ed. Barbara Mauldin. London: Thames & Hudson.

Besant, Annie, and C. W. Leadbeater. 1905. *Thought-Forms*. New York: The Theosophical Publishing Society.

Blavatsky, Helen P. 1877. *Isis Unveiled*. 2 vols. London: The Theosophical Publishing Society.

———. 1888. *The Secret Doctrine*. 2 vols. London: The Theosophical Publishing Society.

———. 1890. *The Key to Theosophy*. London: The Theosophical Publishing Society.

Boeterenbrood, Helen, and Jürgen Prang. 1989. *Van der Mey en het scheep-vaarthuis*. The Hague: Sdu Uitgeverij.

Bossert, Helmut T. 1954. *Folk Art of Europe*. London: A. Zwemmer.

Bradbury, Edward. 1899. "Bells and Their Messages." In *Ecclesiastical Curiosities*, ed. William Andrews. London: William Andrews & Co.

Brandstätter, Christian. 2003. *Wonderful Wiener Werkstätte: Design in Vienna 1903–1932*. London: Thames & Hudson.

Bray, Olive, trans. and ed. 1908. *The Elder or Poetic Edda, Commonly Known as Sæmund's Edda: Part I—the Mythological Poems*. London: The Viking Club.

Brears, Peter. 1981. *Horse Brasses*. London: Country Life Books.

Briscoe, J. Potter. 1899. "Stories about Bells." In *Ecclesiastical Curiosities*, ed. William Andrews. London: William Andrews & Co.

Brill, Edith. 1990. *Life and Traditions on the Cotswolds*. Stroud, England: Alan Sutton Publishing.

Broadwood, Lucy, and J. A. Fuller Maitland. 1893. *English County Songs*. London and New York: The Leadenhall Press; J. B. Cramer & Co.; Simpkin, Marshall, Hamilton, Kent & Co.; and Charles Scribner's Sons.

Brown, R. J. 1993. *English Farmhouses*. London: Robert Hale.

Brown, Stuart J. 1982. *Albion and Crossley Buses in Camera*. Shepperton, England: Ian Allan.

Brunskill, Ronald William. 1987. *Illustrated Handbook of Vernacular Architecture*. London: Faber & Faber.

Bryce, Derek. 1989. *Symbolism of the Celtic Cross*. Felinfach, Wales: Llanerch Publishers.

Buckland, Raymond. 1986. *Buckland's Complete Book of Witchcraft*. St. Paul, Minn.: Llewellyn Publications.

Buckley, Joshua. 2004a. "Keeping Up the Day: Joshua Buckley Interviews Nigel Pennick." *Rûna* 15: 7–10.

———. 2004b. "Keeping Up the Day II: Joshua Buckley Interviews Nigel Pennick." *Rûna* 16:2–5.

Bunn, Ivan. 1982. "'A Devil's Shield . . .' Notes on Suffolk Witch Bottles." *Lantern* 39: 3–7.

Burke, John. 1981. *The English Inn*. London: B. T. Batsford Ltd.

Butcher, D. R. 1972. "The Last Ears of Harvest." *The East Anglian Magazine* 31: 463–65.

Butler, Bill. 1975. *The Definitive Tarot: The Origins of Tarot and Its Inner Meaning*. London: Rider.

Butler, Rohan D'O. 1941. *The Roots of National Socialism: 1783–1933*. London: Faber & Faber.

Campbell, Ewan, and Alan Lane. 1991. "Celtic and Germanic Interaction in Dalriada: The 7th-Century Metalworking Site at Dunadd." In *The Age of Migrating Ideas: Early Medieval Art in Northern Britain and Ireland,* ed. R. Michael Spearman and John Higgitt, 52–63. Edinburgh, Scotland, and Stroud, England: National Museums of Scotland and Alan Sutton Publishing.

Canney, Maurice A. 1926. "The Use of Sand in Magic and Religion." *Man,* January, 13.

Caplan, David, and Gregory Stewart. 1966. *British Trademarks and Symbols*. London: Peter Owen.

Carpenter, Edward. 1920. *Pagan and Christian Creeds: Their Origin and Meaning*. London: George Allen & Unwin.

Carrington, Noel, and Clarke Hutton. 1945. *Popular English Art*. London and New York: Penguin Books.

Chadwick, H. M. 1901. *The Cult of Othing: An Essay on the Ancient Religion of the North*. London: C. J. Clay.

Christian, Roy. 1991. *Well-Dressing in Derbyshire*. Derby, England: Derbyshire Countryside Ltd.

Cirlot, Juan Eduardo. 1962. *A Dictionary of Symbols*. New York: Philosophical Library.

Cole, Malcolm. 1992. *Be Like Daisies: John Ruskin and the Cultivation of Beauty at Whitelands College*. St. Albans, England: The Guild of St. George.

Collingwood, W. G. 1911. "Anglian and Anglo-Danish Sculpture in the East Riding with Addenda to the North Riding." *Yorkshire Archaeological Journal* 21: 255–302.

Collingwood, W. G., and Jón Steffánsson, trans. 1902. *The Life and Death of Cormac The Skald: Being the Icelandic Kormáks-Saga*. Ulverston, England: William Holmes.

Colquhoun, Ithell. 1975. *The Sword of Wisdom*. Sudbury, England: Neville Spearman.

———. 1979. "Notes on the Colouring of the Homer's Golden Chain Diagram." *The Hermetic Journal* 6: 15–17.

Comeno, Mary. 1980. *Gimson and the Barnsleys: Wonderful Furniture of a Commonplace Kind*. New York: Van Nostrand Reinhold.

Commission of the Fryske Akademy. 1956. "DeFryske Flagge." *It Beaken,* Jiergong 18 (2/3): 62–86.

Cooper, Robert L. D. 2006. *Cracking the Freemason's Code*. London: Rider.

Corcoran, Michael, 2000. *Through Streets Broad and Narrow. A History of Dublin Trams*. Eal Shilton, England: Midland Publishing.

Corrie, E. S. 1889. "On Pargeting." *Transactions of the Essex Archaeological Society*, n.s., 3: 203–7.

Corrsin, Stephen D. 1997. *Sword Dancing in Europe: A History*. Enfield Lock, England: Hisarlik Press.

Coulton, G. C. 1914–1915. "Medieval Graffiti, Especially in the Eastern Counties." *Proceedings of the Cambridge Antiquarian Society* 19: 53–62, pls. VI–XVI.

Cowen, Painton. 1979. *Rose Windows*. London: Thames & Hudson.

Crowley, Aleister. 1969. *The Book of Thoth*. New York: Samuel Weiser.

———. 1974. *Gems from the Equinox*. Ed. Israel Regardie. St. Paul, Minn.: Llewellyn Publications.

Cumont, F. 1919. "Mithra ou serapis kosmokrator." *Comptes rendus des séances de l'Académie des Inscriptions et Belles-Lettres*.

Dacombe, Marianne. 1935. *Dorset Up Along and Down Along*. Dorchester, England: Longmans.

D'Apremont, Arnaud. 1995. *Yggdrasill: l'axe de vie des anciens Nordiques*. Combronde, France: Éditions de Janvier.

Davidson, Hilda Ellis. 1960. "The Sword at the Wedding." *Folklore* l (21): 1–18.

———. 1988. *Myths and Symbols in Pagan Europe*. Syracuse, N.Y.: Syracuse University Press.

———. 1993. *The Lost Beliefs of Northern Europe*. London and New York: Routledge.

Davidson, Hilda R. 1943. *The Road to Hel*. Cambridge: Cambridge University Press.

Davídsson, Óláfur. 1903. "Isländische Zauberzeichen und Zauberbücher." *Zeitschrift des Vereins für Volkskunde* 13: 150–67.

Davies, Peter, and Derek Lynch. 2002. *The Routledge Companion to Fascism and the Far Right*. London and New York: Routledge.

Day, George. 1894. "Notes on Essex Dialect and Folk-Lore, with Some Account of the Divining Rod." *The Essex Naturalist* 8: 71–85.

De Vries, Jan. 1956–1957. *Altgermanische Religionsgeschichte*. 2 vols. Berlin: De Gruyter.

Debes, Dietmar. 1956. *Das Ornament: Wesen und Geschichte*. Leipzig, Germany: E. A. Seemann.

Decker, Ronald, and Michael Dummett. 2002. *A History of the Occult Tarot: 1870–1970*. London: Duckworth.

Deneke, Bernward. 1980. *Europäische Volkskunst*. Frankfurt, Germany: Propyläen.

Dennis, George. 1848. *The Cities and Cemeteries of Etruria*. 2 vols. London: John Murray.

Dixon, G. M. 1981. *A Heritage of Anglian Crafts*. Deeping St. James, Peterborough, England: Minimax Books.

Dornsieff, Franz. 1922. *Das Alphabet in Mystik und Magie*. Leipzig, Germany: Teubner.

Downes, Kerry. 1970. *Hawksmoor*. London: Thames & Hudson.

Drucker, Johanna. 1995. *The Alphabetic Labyrinth: The Letters in History and Imagination*. London: Thames & Hudson.

Elliott, Ralph W. V. 1959. *Runes: An Introduction*. Manchester, England: Manchester University Press.

Elworthy, Frederick Thomas. 1895. *The Evil Eye*. London: J. Murray.

Esmond. 1988. "Merchants' Marks, Heraldry, and the Runes." *Odinic Rite Briefing* 79: 3.

Essick, Robert N., and Joseph Viscomi. 1998. *William Blake: Milton a Poem*. London: The William Blake Trust/Tate Gallery.

Evans, E. Estyn. 1957. *Irish Folk Ways*. London: Routledge & Kegan Paul.

Evans, George Ewart. 1965. *Ask the Fellows Who Cut the Hay*. London: Faber and Faber.

Evelyn, John (de Beer, Esmond S.ed.). *Diary and Correspondence*. 6 vols. London: 1894. Oxford: Oxford University Press, 1955.

Fadge, Canon. 1979. *Ye Stone Missal*. Hamilton, Ont., Canada: Acorn.

Fahr-Becker, Gabriele. 1995. *Wiener Werkstätte: 1903–1932*. Cologne, Germany: Taschen.

Fergusson, James. 1893. *A History of Architecture in All Countries*. London: John Murray.

Fevre, Ralph W. 2000. *The Demoralization of Western Culture*. London and New York: Continuum.

Field, Robert. 1996. *Geometrical Patterns from Tiles and Brickwork*. Stradbroke, England: Tarquin.

Flick, Adrian. 1984. "'England's Ghost Story': The Green Man in Literature and Film." *The Symbol* 5: 2–8.

Flowers, Stephen. 1986. *Runes and Magic: Magical Formulaic Elements in the Older Tradition*. New York: Lang.

———. 1989. *The Galdrabók: An Icelandic Grimoire.* York Beach, Maine: Samuel Weiser.

Forbes-Semphill, the Hon. Mrs. 1927. "Music Made Visible." *Illustrated London News,* February 12, 260.

Forby, Robert. 1830. *The Vocabulary of East Anglia.* 2 vols. London: J. B. Nichols and Son.

Franklin, Anna. 2002. *Midsummer: Magical Celebrations of the Summer Solstice.* St. Paul, Minn.: Llewellyn.

Franz, Leonhard. 1943. *Falsche Slawengötter.* Munich: Rudolf M. Rohrer.

Gansohr, Heidi, and Alois Döring. 1984. *Kirchturmhähne.* Cologne, Germany: Rhineland-Verlag.

Gelling, Peter, and Hilda Ellis Davidson. 1971. *The Chariot of the Sun and Other Rites and Symbols in the Northern Bronze Age.* London: Dent.

Gerlach, Martin, ed. 1971. *Primitive and Folk Jewelry.* New York: Dover Publications.

Gettings, Fred. 1981. *Dictionary of Occult, Hermetic, and Alchemical Signs.* London: Routledge & Kegan Paul.

Girling, F. A. 1939. "Pargeting in Suffolk." *Proceedings of the Suffolk Institute of Archæology and Natural History* 23: 202–9.

———. 1962. *English Merchants' Marks.* London: Lion and Unicorn Press.

———. 1964. "Merchants' Marks in Suffolk." *Proceedings of the Suffolk Institute of Archæology* XXIX: 102–26.

Goddard, A. R. 1901. "Nine Men's Morris: An Old Viking Game." In *The Saga-Book of the Viking Club,* 376–85. London.

Goethe, Johann Wolfgang von. 1925. *Faust.* Translated by John Auster. London: Harrap.

Goldsmith, Elizabeth. 1924. *Life Symbols as Related to Sex Symbolism.* New York: G. P. Putnam's Sons.

Gomme, Alice B. 1901. "A Berwickshire Kirn-Dolly." *Folk-Lore* 12 (June): 215–16.

Gouk, Penelope. 1988. *The Ivory Sundials of Nuremberg: 1500–1700.* Cambridge, England: The Whipple Museum.

Green, Deirdre. 1984. "Some Thoughts on Mystical and Esoteric Symbolism." *The Symbol* 2: 3–5.

Grian, Sinead Sula. 1986. *Sun Goddesses of Europe.* Glastonbury, England: Gothic Image.

Griffinhoofe, H. G. 1894. "Breeding Stone." *The Essex Review* 3: 144.

Gwyn. 2002. *Light from the Shadows: A Mythos of Modern Traditional Witchcraft*. Chieveley, England: Capall Bann Publishing.

Hackwood, Frederick W. 1987. *Inns, Ales, and Drinking Customs of Old England*. London: Bracken Books.

Haigh, Daniel Henry. 1866. "Yorkshire Dials." *Yorkshire Archaeological Journal*: 134–222.

Haigh, Diane. 1995. *Baillie Scott: The Artistic House*. London: Academy Editions.

Hall, Manly P. 1928. *An Encyclopedic Outline of Masonic, Hermetic, Qabbalistic, and Rosicrucian Symbolical Philosophy*. Los Angeles, Calif.: Philosophical Research Society.

Hallman, Frithjof. 1988. *Labyrinthe und Trojaburgen*. Bonn, Germany: Mannus Bibliothek NF Band 29.

Hamill, John. 1986. *The Craft: A History of English Freemasonry*. London: Crucible.

Hamilton, Jean. 1988. *Playing Cards in the Victoria and Albert Museum*. London: Her Majesty's Stationery Office.

Harley, Laurence S. 1952. "Graffiti in Essex." *The Essex Naturalist* 29: 1–8.

Harper, Charles G. 1931. *Queer Things about London*. London: Cecil Palmer.

Harvey, Michael, and Rae Compton. 1978. *Fisherman Knitting*. Risborough, England: Shire Publications, Prince's.

Haseloff, Günther. 1979. *Kunststile des frühen Mittelalters*. Stuttgart, Germany: Württembergisches Landesmuseum Stuttgart.

Hayes, R. H., and J. G. Rutter. 1972. *Cruck-Framed Buildings of Ryedale and Eskdale*. Scarborough, England: Scarborough Archaeological and Historical Society.

Haynes, Edmund Sidney Pollock. 1906. *Religious Persecution: A Study in Political Psychology*. London: Watts & Co.

Heilbron, John L. 1999. *The Sun in the Church: Cathedrals as Solar Observatories*. Cambridge, Mass.: Harvard University Press.

Herrmann, Paul. 1929. *Das altgermanische Priesterwesen*. Jena, Germany: Eugen Diederichs.

Heseltine, Peter. 2006. *A Bestiary of Brass*. Wymeswold, England: Heart of Albion Press.

Hieronymussen, Paul, and Aage Strüwing. 1967. *Orders, Medals, and Decorations of Britain and Europe*. London: Blandford Press.

Hohenzollern, Wilhelm (Kaiser Wilhelm II). 1934. *Die chinesische Monade: Ihre Geschichte und ihre Deutung*. Leipzig, Germany: Koehler & Amerlang.

Hole, Christina. 1977. "Protective Symbols in the Home." In *Symbols of Power,* ed. H. R. Ellis-Davidson. London: The Folklore Society.

Holme, Charles, ed. 1906. *Old English Country Cottages. The Studio,* special winter number 1906–1907, London, Paris, and New York: The Studio.

Hone, William. 1827. *The Every-Day Book.* 2 vols. London: Hunt and Clarke.

Hooper, Bari. 2002. "Gog and Magog at Saffron Walden." *3rd Stone* 43: 62–63.

Howes, Michael. 1975. *Amulets.* New York: St. Martin's Press.

Hughes, Harold, and Herbert L. North. 1924. *The Old Churches of Snowdonia.* Bangor, Wales: privately published.

Hutton, Ronald. 1996. *The Stations of the Sun: A History of the Ritual Year in Britain.* Oxford: Oxford University Press.

Jennings, Celia, ed. 1993. *Patterns for Suffolk Buildings: A Simple Design Guide.* Lavenham, England: Suffolk Building Preservation Trust.

Jensen, K. Frank. 1975. *Tarot.* Copenhangen: Strubes Forlag.

———. 1985. *The Prophetic Cards: A Catalog of Cards for Fortune-Telling.* Roskilde, Demark: Ouroboros.

———. 1990. *110 More Fortune-Telling Decks.* Vol. 2 of *The Prophetic Cards.* Roskilde, Denmark: Ouroboros.

———. 1991. *Magiske runer.* Copenhagen: Sphinx.

———. 1996. *184 More Cartomancy Decks.* Vol. 3 of *The Prophetic Cards.* Roskilde, Denmark: Ouroboros.

Jewitt, Llewellyn. 1984. "A Few Words on the Fylfot." *The Symbol* 5. Reprint from *Yorkshire Notes and Queries* 1 (1888).

Johns, June. 1969. *King of the Witches: The World of Alex Sanders.* London: Peter Davies.

Johnston, J. A. 1983. *Symbolism in Keltic Art.* Edinburgh: Keltia Publications.

Johnston, Walter. 1912. *Byways in British Archaeology.* Cambridge: Cambridge University Press.

Jones, Barbara. 1951. *The Unsophisticated Arts.* London: The Architectural Press.

Jones, Bernard E. 1956. *Freemasons' Guide and Compendium.* London: Harrap.

Jones, Prudence. 1982. *Eight and Nine: Sacred Numbers of Sun and Moon in the Pagan North.* Fenris-Wolf Pagan Paper #2. Bar Hill, England: Fenris-Wolf.

———. 1991a. *A "House" System from Viking Europe.* Bar Hill, England: Fenris-Wolf.

———. 1991b. *Northern Myths of the Constellations.* Bar Hill, England: Fenris-Wolf.

Jones, Prudence, and Nigel Pennick. 1995. *A History of Pagan Europe*. London: Routledge.

Jones, Sydney R. 1912. *The Village Homes of England*. London: The Studio.

Kandinsky, Wassily. 1977. *Concerning the Spiritual in Art*. Translated by M. T. H. Sadler. New York: Dover Publications.

Jung, Carl G. 1959. *The Archetypes and the Collective Unconscious*. Translated by R. F. C. Hull. Princeton, N.J.: Princeton University Press.

———, ed. 1964. *Man and His Symbols*. London: Aldus.

Kearns, Rev. J. F. 2001. *Silpa Sastra*. Cambridge, England: The Institute of Experimental Geomancy.

Kern, Hermann. 1983. *Labyrinthe*. Munich, Germany: Prestel.

———. 2000. *Through the Labyrinth*. Translated, edited, and with notes and additional material by Jeff Saward. Munich, Germany: Prestel.

Kieckheffer, Richard. 1989. *Magic in the Middle Ages*. Cambridge: Cambridge University Press.

Kimmis, Jim. 1984. "The Bell and the Grail." *The Symbol* 4: 3–5.

Koch, Rudolf. 1930. *The Book of Signs*. London: The First Edition Club.

Köstlin, Konrad. 1977. "Feudale Identität und dogmatisierte Volkultur." *Zeitschrift für Volkskunde* 73: 216–33.

Krause, Rhett. 1996. "Traditional and Invented Sword Locks." *Rattle Up My Boys* 6 (1) Spring: 1–7.

Krauss, F. 1944. "Die Prora an der Tiberinsel." *Mitteilungen des Deutschen Archäolgigischen Insituts, Römische Abteilung* 59: 159–65.

Kruft, Hanno-Walter. 1985. *Geschichte der Architekturtheorie: Von der Antike bis zur Gegenwart*. Munich: C. H. Beck'sche Verlagsbuchhandlung.

Kummer, Siegfried Adolf. 1932. *Die heilige Runenmacht*. Hamburg, Germany: Uranus-Verlag.

———. 1933. *Runen-Magie*. Dresden, Germany: Hartmann.

Künkel, Hans. 1922. *Das grosse Jahr*. Jena, Germany: Eugen Diederichs.

Laing, Gordon J. 1931. *Survivals of Roman Religion*. London: George G. Harrap & Co.

Laing, L. 1973. "The Mote of Mark." *Current Archaeology* 39: 121–25.

Lambert, Margaret, and Enid Marx. 1989. *English Popular Art*. London: Merlin Press.

Lambeth, M. 1969. *A Golden Dolly: The Art, Mystery, and History of Corn Dollies*. London: John Baker.

Larner, Christina. 1984. *Witchcraft and Religion: The Politics of Popular Belief*. Oxford, England: Blackwell.

Larrington, Carolyne, trans. 1996. *The Poetic Edda*. Oxford & New York: Oxford University Press.

Larwood, Jacob, and John Camden Hotten. 1985. *English Inn Signs: A Revised and Modernized Version of* The History of Signboards. New York: Arco Publishing. (Orig. pub. 1866.)

Lauweriks, Johannes Ludovicus Mathieu. 1925. *De houtsneden van K.P.C de Bazel*. Amsterdam: S. L. van Looy.

Laver, Henry. 1907. "Pargetting." *Transactions of the Essex Archaeological Society*, n.s., 10: 73–78.

Lawrence, David. 2000. *A Logo for London*. Harrow Weald, England: Capital Transport Publishing.

Leadbeater, C. W. 1903. *Man Visible and Invisible*. New York: John Lane.

Leather, Ella Mary. 1912. *The Folk-Lore of Herefordshire*. Hereford, England: Jakeman and Carver; London: Sidgwick and Jackson.

Lebech, Mogens. 1969. *Fra runestav til almanak*. Copenhagen: Theijls.

Leboff, David. 2002. *The Underground Stations of Leslie Green*. London: Capital Transport Publishing.

Leeson, R. A. 1971. *United We Stand: An Illustrated Account of Trade Union Emblems*. London: Adams and Dart.

Legeza, Laszlo. 1975. *Tao Magic: The Secret Language of Diagrams and Calligraphy*. London: Thames & Hudson.

Lethaby, William Richard. 1891. *Architecture: Mysticism and Myth*. London: The Architectural Press.

———. 1893. *Leadwork, Old and Ornamental and for the Most Part English*. London: The Architectural Press.

———. 1913. "Art and Workmanship." *The Imprint* 1: 1–3.

Lewery, A. J. 1974. *Narrow Boat Painting*. Newton Abbot, England: David and Charles.

———. 1991. *Popular Art: Past and Present*. Newton Abbot, England: David and Charles.

Lewery, Tony. 1996. *Flowers Afloat: Artists of the Canals*. Newton Abbot, England: David and Charles.

Linden, Stanton J., ed. 2003. *The Alchemy Reader*. Cambridge: Cambridge University Press.

Lipman, Jean, and Eve Meulendyke. 1951. *Techniques in American Folk Decoration*. London: Constable.

Lippert, Reinhold. 1994. *Osterbrunnen in der Fränkischen Schweiz*. Ebermannstadt, Germany: Lippert Verlag.

Lippman, Deborah, and Paul Colin. 1974. *How To Make Amulets, Charms, and Talismans: What They Mean and How To Use Them.* Sydney, Auckland, Toronto, and Johannesburg: Michael Dempsey.

List, Guido. 1910. *Die Bilderschrift der Ario-Germanen (Ario-Germanische Hieroglyphik).* 2 vols. Vienna: Guido von List Verlag.

Lundqvist, Sune. 1923. "Hednatemplet i Uppsala." *Fornvännen* 18: 85–118.

MacDonald, M. Irwin. 1912. "The Fairy Faith and Pictured Music of Pamela Colman Smith." *The Craftsman* 23: 33.

Machen, Arthur. 1915. *The Bowmen and Other Legends of the War.* London: Simkin, Marshall, Hamilton, Kent, & Co.

Macmurdo, A. H., ed. 1892. *Plain Handicrafts: Being Essays by Artists Setting Forth the Principles of Design and Established Methods of Craftsmanship.* London.

Maddren, Victoria. 1992. *Who Was Jack O'Legs?* Baldock, England: Egon Publishers.

Mair, Craig. 1988. *Mercat Cross and Tolbooth.* Edinburgh: John Donald Publishers.

Manker, Ernst. 1938. *Die lappische Zaubertrommel 1.* Stockholm: Acta Lapponica 1.

———. 1950. *Die lappische Zaubertrommel 2.* Stockholm: Acta Lapponica 6.

Mann, Ludovic MacLellan. 1915. *Archaic Sculpturings.* Edinburgh: William Hodge.

Marby, Friedrich Bernhard. 1931. *Runenschrift, Runenwort, Runengymnastik.* Stuttgart, Germany: Marby-Runen-Bücherei.

March, H. Colley. 1899. "Dorset Folk-Lore Collected in 1897." *Folk-Lore* 10: 483.

Marta, Roberto. 1990. *Architettura Romana: Techniche costruttive e forme architettoniche del mondo Romano.* Rome: Edizioni Kappa.

Martin, Eugène. 1903–1904. "Le coq du clocher." *Memoires de l'Academie de Stanislas* 6: 1, 6.

Mason, Hugo. 2001. *All Saints' Church, Brockhampton, Herefordshire.* Brockhampton, England: Brockhampton Parochial Church Council.

Masters, David. 1955. *The Plimsoll Mark.* London: Cassell.

Matthäus, Hartmut. 1987. *Der Arzt in Römischer Zeit.* Aalen, Germany: Gesellschaft für Vor- und Frühgeschichte in Württemberg und Hohenzollern.

Matthews, John, and Caitlín Matthews. 1995. *British and Irish Mythology.* London: Diamond Books.

Matthews, William Henry. 1922. *Mazes and Labyrinths: A General Account of Their History and Developments*. London: Longmans, Green, and Co.

McFadzean, Patrick. 1999. *Vastu Vidya: Studies in Indian Geomancy*. Cambridge, England: The Institute of Experimental Geomancy.

McLean, Adam. 1979. "The Golden Chain of Homer: Commentary." *The Hermetic Journal* 4: 21–24.

Meates, Lt. Col. G. W. 1963. *Lullingstone Roman Villa, Kent*. London: Her Majesty's Stationery Office.

Meltzer, Albert. 1976. *The Anarchists in London, 1935–1955*. Sanday, Scotland: Cienfuegos Press.

Mockridge, Patricia, and Philip Mockridge. 1990. *Weathervanes of Great Britain*. London: Robert Hale.

Monson-Fitzjohn, Gilbert John. 1926. *Quaint Signs of Olde Inns*. London: Herbert Jenkins.

Mosse, George L. 1975. *The Nationalization of the Masses: Political Symbolism and Mass Movements from the Napoleonic Wars through the Third Reich*. Ithaca, N.Y.: Cornell University Press.

Mössinger, Friedrich. 1938a. "Die Dorflinde als Weltbaum." *Germanien*, 388–96.

———. 1938b. "Maibaum, Dorflinde, Weihnachtsbaum." *Germanien*, 145–55.

———. 1940. "Baumtanz und Trojaburg." *Germanien*, 282–89.

Murray, Colin. 1979. "Ogham Chart." *Lug nassadh lammas*. London: The Golden Section Order, The Bardic Chair of Caer Llyndain, 3.

Naylor, Peter, and Lindsey Porter. 2002. *Well Dressing*. Ashbourne, England: Landmark Publishing.

Nevinson, J. L. 1966–1968. "The Embroidery Patterns of Thomas Trevelyon." *Walpole Society* 41: 1–38.

Newman, L. F. 1930. "Mummers' Play from Middlesex." *Folk-Lore* 41: 95–98.

Nicolaysen, Nicolay. 1882. *Langskibet fra Gokstad*. Christiania, Denmark: Alb. Cammermeyer.

Norbury, James. 1973. *Traditional Knitting Patterns from Scandinavia, the British Isles, France, Italy, and Other European Countries*. New York: Dover Publications.

North, C. N. McIntyre. 1881. *Leabhar comunn nam fion ghael: The Book of the Club of True Highlanders*, vol. 1. London: The Club of True Highlanders.

Novati, Francesco. 1905. "'Li dis du koc' di Jean de Condé." *Studi Medievali* 1: 497.

Nylén, Erik, and Jan Peter Lamm. 1981. *Bildsteine auf Gotland*. Neumünster, Germany: Karl Wachholz Verlag.

Orme, Nicholas. 1986. *Exeter Cathedral as It Was: 1050–1550*. Exeter, England: Devon Books.

Osborn, Marijane, and Stella Longland. 1982. *Rune Games*. London: Routledge & Kegan Paul.

Paine, Sheila. 2004. *Amulets: A World of Secret Powers, Charms, and Magic*. London: Thames & Hudson.

Palmer, Roy. 1992. *The Folklore of Hereford and Worcester*. Little Logaston, England: Logaston Press.

———. 2004. *The Folklore of Shropshire*. Little Logaston, England: Logaston Press.

Panciroli, Guido. 1606. *Notitia dignitatum*. Lyon, France: Pierre Fradin.

Panofsky, Erwin. 1955. *Meaning in the Visual Arts*. Chicago: University of Chicago Press.

Parker, John Henry. 1845. *A Glossary of Terms Used in Grecian, Roman, Italian, and Gothic Architecture*. London: David Bogue.

Parsons, Melinda Boyd. 1987. "Mysticism in London: The 'Golden Dawn,' Synaesthesia, and 'Psychic Automatism' in the Art of Pamela Colman Smith." In *The Spiritual Image in Modern Art,* ed. Kathleen J. Regier. Wheaton, Madras, London: The Theosophical Publishing House.

Paulsen, Peter, and Helga Schach-Dörges. 1972. *Holzhandwerk der Alamannen*. Stuttgart, Germany: Verlag W. Kohlhammer.

Pearson, Michael. 1984. *Michael Pearson's Traditional Knitting: Aran, Fair Isle, and Fisher Ganseys*. London: Collins.

Peesch, Reinhard. 1983. *The Ornament in European Folk Art*. London: Alpine Fine Arts.

Pennick, Nigel. 1972. "Organic Metaphysics." *Arcana,* December, 4–23.

———. 1974a. *Caerdroia: Ancient Turf, Stone, and Pavement Mazes*. Trumpington, England: Megalithic Visions Etcetera.

———. 1974b. *The Mysteries of King's College Chapel*. Cambridge, England: Cokaygne Press.

———. 1974c. *Runic*. Trumpington, England: Megalithic Visions Etcetera.

———. 1975. *The Swastika*. Megalithic Visions Antiquarian Papers, no. 10, Bar Hill, England: Fenris-Wolf.

———. 1978. *Ogham and Runic: Magical Writing of Old Britain and Northern Europe*. Bar Hill, England: Fenris-Wolf.

———. 1979a. *The Ancient Science of Geomancy*. London: Thames & Hudson.

———. 1979b. *The Swastika*. Bar Hill, England: Fenris-Wolf.

———. 1980a. *Daddy Witch and Old Mother Redcap: Survivals of the Old Craft under Victorian Christendom*. Bar Hill, England: Fenris-Wolf Publications.

———, ed. 1980b. *The Grand Mystery: Being a Reprint of Two Tracts of the Eighteenth Century on the Secrets of Free-Masonry*. Bar Hill, England: Fenris-Wolf.

———. 1980c. *Sacred Geometry: Symbolism and Purpose in Religious Structures*. Wellingborough, England: Aquarian Press.

———. 1982. *Vintana: Geomancy and Astrology in Madagascar*. Cambridge, England: The Institute of Geomantic Research.

———. 1983. "Triangular Lodge, Rushton." *The Symbol* 1: 2–6.

———. 1984a. "Bell Lore." *The Symbol* 3: 12–17.

———. 1984b. *Labyrinths: Their Geomancy and Symbolism*. Bar Hill, England: Runestaff.

———. 1984c. *Pagan Prophecy and Play in Northern Europe*. Bar Hill, England: Runestaff.

———. 1985a. *The Cosmic Axis*. Bar Hill, England: Runestaff.

———. 1985b. *Runestaves and Oghams*. Bar Hill, England: Runestaff.

———. 1987. *Einst war uns die Erde Heilig*. Waldeck-Dehringhausen, Germany: Felicitas-Hübner Verlag.

———. 1988. *Traditional Board Games of Northern Europe*. Bar Hill, England: Valknut Productions.

———. 1989a. *Games of the Gods*. London: Rider.

———. 1989b. *Practical Magic in the Northern Tradition*. Wellingborough, England: The Aquarian Press.

———. 1990a. *Mazes and Labyrinths*. London: Robert Hale.

———. 1990b. *Das Runenorakel*. With rune cards by Hermann Haindl. Frankfurt, Germany: Droemer Knaur.

———. 1990c. *Runic Astrology: Starcraft and Timekeeping in the Northern Tradition*. Wellingborough, England: Aquarian Press.

———. 1991a. *Celtic Art in the Northern Tradition*. Bar Hill, England: Nideck.

———. 1991b. *The Secret Lore of Runes and Other Ancient Alphabets*. London: Rider.

———. 1992a. "The Reality Censors: The World as Real Estate." *Fortean Times* 62 (April):45–46.

———. 1992b. *Rune Magic: The History and Practice of Ancient Runic Traditions*. London: Aquarian/Thorsons.

———. 1993a. *Anima Loci*. Bar Hill, England: The Way of the Eight Winds/ Nideck.

———. 1993b. "The Magic of Labyrinths." *The Occult Observer* 2 (4): 10–14.

———. 1993c. *Wayland's House*. Bar Hill, England: The Way of the Eight Winds/Nideck.

———. 1995a. *The Inner Mysteries of the Goths: Rune-Lore and Secret Wisdom of the Northern Tradition*. Chieveley, England: Capall Bann Publishing.

———. 1995b. *Secrets of East Anglian Magic*. London: Hale.

———. 1995c. *The Oracle of Geomancy. The Divinatory Arts of Raml, Geomantia, Sikidy and I Ching*. Chieveley, England: Capall Bann Publishing.

———. 1996a. *Celtic Sacred Landscapes*. London: Thames & Hudson.

———. 1996b. *Secret Signs, Symbols, and Sigils*. Chieveley, England: Capall Bann Publishing.

———. 1997a. *The Celtic Cross: An Illustrated History and Celebration*. London: Blandford.

———. 1997b. *The Celtic Saints*. London: Thorsons.

———. 1997c. *Dragons of the West*. Chieveley, England: Capall Bann Publishing.

———. 1997d. *Earth Harmony: Places of Power, Holiness, and Healing.* 2nd ed. Chieveley, England: Capall Bann Publishing.

———. 1999a. *Beginnings: Geomancy, Builders' Rites, and Electional Astrology in the European Tradition*. Chieveley, England: Capall Bann Publishing.

———. 1999b. *The Complete Illustrated Guide to Runes*. Shaftesbury, England: Element Books.

———. 2000a. *Ogham and Coelbren: Keys to the Celtic Mysteries*. Chieveley, England: Capall Bann Publishing.

———. 2000b. *On Building in the European Tradition*. Cambridge, England: The Library of the European Tradition.

———. 2000c. *Pargetting in Eastern England*. Cambridge, England: The Library of the European Tradition.

———. 2001. *On the Spiritual Arts and Crafts: Practising the Ancient Skills and Wisdom of Europe*. Cambridge, England: The Library of the European Tradition.

———. 2002a. "The Goddess Zisa." *Tyr* 1: 107–9.

———. 2002b. *Masterworks: Arts and Crafts of Traditional Buildings in Northern Europe*. Wymeswold, England: Heart of Albion Press.

———. 2002c. *The Power Within: The Way of the Warrior and the Martial Arts in the European Tradition*. Chieveley, England: Capall Bann Publishing.

———. 2003a. "Lux e Tenebris: Das Licht als Brücke zum Immateriellen." Translated by Eberhard Hierse. *Hagia Chora* 17: 80–83.

———. 2003b. "The Religion of Northern Europe." *The Times World Religions,* 44–51.

———. 2004a. *Secrets of East Anglian Magic.* Milverton, England: Capall Bann Publishing.

———. 2004b. *Threshold and Hearthstone Patterns.* Bar Hill, England: Old England House.

———. 2005a. *Natural Magic.* Earl Shilton, England: Lear Books.

———. 2005b. *The Sacred Art of Geometry: Temples of the Phoenix.* Bar Hill, England: Spiritual Arts & Crafts Publishing.

———. 2006a. *The Eldritch World.* Earl Shilton, England: Lear Books.

———. 2006b. *Folk-Lore of East Anglia and Adjoining Counties.* Bar Hill, England: Spiritual Arts & Crafts Publishing.

———. 2006c. "Geomancers." *Quintessentially* 10: 54–65.

———. 2006d. *The Spiritual Arts and Crafts.* Bar Hill, England: Spiritual Arts & Crafts Publishing.

Pennick, Nigel, and Helen Field. 2003. *A Book of Beasts.* Milverton, England: Capall Bann Publishing.

———. 2004. *Muses and Fates.* Milverton, England: Capall Bann Publishing.

Pennick, Rupert. 1984. "The Secret Vehm." *The Symbol* 3: 20–23.

Pentikäinen, Juha. 1987. "The Shamanic Drum as Cognitive Map." In *Mythology and the Cosmic Order,* ed. René Gothóni and Juha Pentikäinen. *Studia Fennica* 32: 17–36.

Petrie, Sir Flinders. 1930. *Decorative Patterns of the Ancient World.* London: Studio Editions.

Piggot, John. 1870. "On the Tau Cross and Fylfot." *The East Anglian* 4: 9.

———. 1878. "A Note on 'Pargetting.'" *Transactions of the Essex Archaeological Society* 5: 73–78. (With reference to a fine example at Wyvenhoe, Essex.)

Pittaway, Andy, and Bernard Scofield. 1976a. *The Complete Country Bizarre.* London: Astragal.

———. 1976b. *Country Bazaar: A Handbook of Country Pleasures.* London: Fontana.

Porter, Enid. 1969. *Cambridgeshire Customs and Folklore.* London: Routledge & Kegan Paul.

Pritchard, Violet. 1967. *English Medieval Graffiti.* Cambridge: Cambridge University Press.

Propping, Walter. 1935. "Das 'dag' zeichen am Niedersächsischen Bauernhaus." *Germanien*, 143–46.

Rabelais, François. 1927. *The Complete Works of Doctor François Rabelias Abstractor of the Quintessence: Being an Account of the Inestimable Life of the Great Gargantua, and of the Heroic Deeds, Sayings and Marvellous Voyages of his Son The Good Pantagruel*. 2 vols. Translated by Sir Thomas Urquhart and Peter Motteux. London: John Lane & The Bodley Head.

Raglan, Lady. 1939. "The 'Green Man' in Church Architecture." *Folk-Lore* 50: 45–57.

Ranke, K. 1969. "Orale und literale Kontinuität." In *Kontinuität? Geschichtlichkeit und Dauer als volkskundliches Problem: Festschrift Hans Moser*. Edited by H. Bausinger and W. Brückner. Berlin: E. Schmidt.

Reed, John. 2000. *London Buses: A Brief History*. Harrow Weald, England: Capital Transport Publishing.

Regardie, Israel. 1977. *How to Make and Use Talismans*. Wellingborough, England: Aquarian Press.

Regier, Kathleen J., ed. 1987. *The Spiritual Image in Modern Art*. Wheaton, Ill.: The Theosophical Publishing House.

Reuter, Otto Sigfrid. 1934. *Germanische Himmelskunde*. Munich: Lehmann.

———. 1987. *Sky Lore of the North*. Translated by Michael Behrend. Bar Hill, England: The Earthlore Institute.

Ritzer, George. 1992. *The McDonaldization of Society*. London: Sage.

Robertson, Pamela. 1995. *Charles Rennie Mackintosh: Art is the Flower*. London: Pavilion Books.

Romilly Allen, J. 1904. *Celtic Art in Pagan and Christian Times*. London: Methuen.

Rouse, W. H. D. 1899. "Christmas Mummers at Rugby." *Folk-Lore* 10: 186–94.

Rudbeck, Olaf Sr. 1702. *Atland eller Manhem* (Norcopensis, Andreas, contemporary Latin translation, *Atlantica*). Uppsala, Sweden.

Rushen, Joyce. 1984. "Folklore and Witchcraft in Tudor and Stuart England." *Popular Archaeology*, April, 35.

Ruskin, John. 1906. *The Queen of the Air*. London: George Allen.

Ryan M. 1991. "Links between Anglo-Saxon and Irish Early Medieval Art: Some Evidence in Metalwork." In *Studies in Insular Art and Archaeology*. Edited by Catherine Karkov and Robert T. Farrell. Oxford, Ohio: American Early Medieval Studies.

Saxo Grammaticus. 1905. *The Nine Books of the Danish History of Saxo Grammaticus*. Translated by Oliver Elton. New York: Norroena Society.

Schefferus, Johannes. 1673. *Lapponia, id est Regionis Lapponum et Gentis Nova et Verissima Descriptio* . . . . Frankfurt, Germany: Christian Wolff.

Scheuermann, Wilhelm. 1933. *Woher kommt das Hakenkreuz?* Berlin: Rowohlt.

Schmidt, Friedrich Heinz. 1936. *Osterbräuche*. Leipzig, Germany: Bibliographisches Institut.

Schnippel, E. 1926. "Die Englischen Kalendarstäbe." *Leipziger Beiträge zur Englischen Philologie,* 24–105.

Schoenmaekers, Mathieu H. J. 1915. *Het nieuwe wereldbeeld*. Bussum, the Netherlands: Van Dishoeck.

Schwabe, K. H., and G. Rother. 1985. *Angewandte Baubiologie: Biespiele aus der Praxis*. Waldeck-Dehringhausen, Germany: Felicitas-Hübner Verlag.

Schwedt, Herbert, Elke Schwedt, and Martin Blümke. 1984. *Masken und Maskenschnitzer der Schwäbisch-Allemannischen Fasnacht*. Stuttgart, Germany: Konrad Thiess Verlag.

Scott, Mackay Hugh Baillie. 1906. *Houses and Gardens*. London: George Newnes.

———. 1909. "Ideals in Buildings, False and True." In *The Arts Connected with Building,* ed. R. Weir Schulz. London: Batsford.

Shaftesbury, Edmund. 1943. *Universal Magnetism: A Private Training Course in the Magnetic Control of Others by the Most Powerful of All Known Methods*. Marple, England: Psychology Publishing Company.

Shermer, David. 1971. *Blackshirts: Fascism in Britain*. New York: Ballantine.

Sieber, Siegfried. 1936. "Ein Trojaburg in Pommern." *Germanien,* 83–86.

Silberer, Herbert. 1971. *Problems of Mysticism and Its Symbolism*. New York: Moffat, Yard, & Co.

Simpson, H. F. Morland. 1895. "Notes on a Swedish Staff-Calendar, Presented to the Museum by the Hon. John Abercrombie, FSA Scot, Dated 1710." *Proceedings of the Society of Antiquaries of Scotland* 29: 234–40.

Simpson, W. Douglas. 1933. "Edzell Castle: Sculptures in the Pleasaunce." *Transactions of the Edinburgh Architectural Association,* 17–24.

———. 1965. *The Ancient Stones of Scotland*. London: Robert Hale.

Skinner, Frederick George. 1967. *Weights and Measures*. London: Her Majesty's Stationery Office.

Skinner, Stephen. 1980. *Terrestrial Astrology: Divination by Geomancy*. London: Routledge & Kegan Paul.

Smith, Pamela Colman. 1899. *Annancy Stories*. New York: R. H. Russell.

Spamer, Adolf. 1935. *Die Deutsche Volkskunde*. Leipzig, Germany: Bibliographisches Institut.

Spence, Lewis. 1928. *The Mysteries of Britain*. London: Rider.

———. 1941. *The Occult Causes of the Present War*. London, New York, Melbourne: Rider.

———. 1947. *Myth and Ritual in Dance, Game, and Rhyme*. London: Watts & Co.

———. 1980. *Medieval Pilgrim Badges from Norfolk*. Norwich, England: Norfolk Museums Service.

Stansill, Peter, and David Zane Mairowitz. 1971. *BAMN: Outlaw Manifestos and Ephemera 1965–70*. Harmondsworth, England: Penguin Books.

Stretton, Clement E. 1909. "The L. & N. W. Railway Company's Diamond or Trade Mark." *Melton Mowbray Times,* February 19.

Strygell, Anna-Lisa. 1974. "Kyrkans Teken och Årets Gång." *Finnska fornminnesföreningens tidskrift* 77:46.

Suster, Gerald. 1990. *The Truth about the Tarot*. London: Skoob Books Publishing.

Swanton, Michael. 1979. *Roof-Bosses and Corbels of Exeter Cathedral*. Exeter, England: The Dean & Chapter of Exeter Cathedral.

Symon, John. 1979. "Gargoyle Evokation." *The Hermetic Journal* 5: 19–21.

Taplin, Eric. 1994. *Near to Revolution: The Liverpool General Transport Strike of 1911*. Liverpool, England: The Bluecoat Press.

Taylor, Rev. Stephen. 2006. *The Fylfot File*. Cambridge, England: Perfect Publishers.

Tegtmeier, Ralph. 1988. *Runen: Alphabet der Erkenntnis*. Frankfurt, Germany: Urania Verlag.

Theophilus. 1979. *On Divers Arts*. Translated by John G. Hawthorne and Cyril Stanley Smith. New York: Dover Publications.

Thompson, Ernest. 1948. *The History of Modern Spiritualism*. Manchester, England: Two Worlds Publishing Company.

Thompson, Gladys. 1955. *Guernsey Patterns*. London: Batsford.

Thorsson, Edred. 1984. *Futhark: A Handbook of Rune Magic*. York Beach, Maine: Samuel Weiser.

———. 1992. *Northern Magic*. St. Paul, Minn.: Llewellyn.

———. 1993. *Green Rûna: The Runemaster's Notebook; Shorter Works of Edred Thorsson*. Vol. 1 (1978–1985). Austin, Tex.: Runa-Raven Press.

Ticehurst, N. F. 1937. "The Swan-Marks of Cambridgeshire and Huntingdonshire." *The Transactions of the Cambridgeshire and Huntingdonshire Archaeological Society* 5: 121–76.

Tickell, Thomas. 1751. *The Minor Poets: Or the Works of the Most Celebrated Authors, of Whose Writings There Are but Small Remains*. 2 vols. Dublin: Wilson, Exshaw, Esdall, James, Price & Williamson.

Tod, D. A. N. 1935. "Mumming Plays." *Folk-Lore* 46: 361–74.

Trinkūnas, Jonas, ed. 1999. *Of Gods and Holidays: The Baltic Heritage*. Vilnius, Lithuania: Tvermė.

Unterman, Alan. 1991. *Dictionary of Jewish Lore and Legend*. London: Thames & Hudson.

Usener, Hermann. 1905. "Sol Invictus." *Rheinisches Museum für Philologie*, LX, 465-491.

Valentine, Basil. 1610. *Artis auriferae quam chemiam vocant*. 3 vols. Basel, Switzerland: Perna.

Valentine, Mark. 1984. "The Red Lion: From Royal Duke to Revolutionaries." *The Symbol* 4: 16–20.

Van der Klift-Tellegen, Henriette. 1987. *Knitting from the Netherlands: Traditional Dutch Fishermen's Sweaters*. London: Dryad Press, Ltd.

Van Duyn, Roel. 1972. *Message of a Wise Kabouter*. Translated by Hubert Hoskins. London: Duckworth.

Van Loghem, J. B. 1918. "De Eenheit in de komende Kunst." *Wendingen* 1 (5): 15–16.

Vaughan, Thomas. 1650. *Coelum Terrae, or the Magician's Heavenly Chaos*. London: T. W. for H. B.

Vernaliken, Theodor. 1858. *Alpensagen: Volksüberlieferungen aus der Schweiz*. Vienna: Wien.

Villiers, Elizabeth. 1923. *The Mascot Book*. London: T. Werner Laurie.

Von Negelein, Julius. 1906. *Germanische Mythologie*. Leipzig, Germany: Teubner.

Von Zaborsky, Oskar. 1936. *Urväter-Erbe in Deutscher Volkskunst*. Leipzig, Germany: Koehler & Amerlang.

Voysey, Charles Francis Annesley. 1909. "Ideas in Things." In *The Arts Connected with Building: Lectures on Craftsmanship and Design, Delivered at Carpenters' Hall, London Wall, for the Worshipful Company of Carpenters*. London.

Waite, Arthur Edward. 1887. *The Real History of the Rosicrucians*. London: George Redway.

Ward, Artemus [Charles Farrar Browne]. 1901. *The Complete Works of Artemus Ward*. London: Chatto & Windus.

Warde-Fowler, William. 1911. *The Religious Experience of the Roman People*. London: Macmillian.

Weiser-Aal, Lily. 1947. "Magiske tegn på Norske trekar?" *By og byd årbok,* 117–44.

Wendel, Charles H. 1995. *American Automobile Trademarks: 1900–1960.* Osceola, Wisc.: Motorbooks International.

Whinney, Margaret. 1971. *Wren.* London: Thames & Hudson.

Whittick, Arnold. 1971. *Symbols: Signs and the Meaning and Uses in Design.* London: Leonard Hill.

Widnall, Samuel Page. 1892. *Gossiping through the Streets of Cambridge.* Grantchester, England: privately published.

Wildbur, Peter. 1966. *Trademarks: A Handbook of International Designs.* London: Studi Vista.

Wilgus, D. K. 1973. "The Text Is the Thing." *Journal of American Folklore* 86: 241–52.

Wilkinson, Richard H. 1994. *Symbol and Magic in Egyptian Art.* London: Thames & Hudson.

Willett, Fred. 1980. "Pargetting." *Bygones* 5: 6–33.

Willis, Robert, and John Willis Clark. 1886. *The Architectural History of the University of Cambridge,* 3 vols. Cambridge: Cambridge University Press.

Wilser, Ludwig. 1918. *Das Hakenkreuz nach Ursprung, Vorkommen, und Bedeutung.* Zeitz, Germany: Sis-Verlag.

Wilson, Geoffrey. 1976. *The Old Telegraphs.* London and Chichester, England: Phillimore.

Wilson, Robert J. 1976. *Roses and Castles.* Stoke Bruerne, England: The Waterways Museum.

Wirth, Herman. 1928. *Der Aufgang der Menschheit.* Jena, Germany: Eugen Diederichs.

———. 1931–1936. *Die Heilige Urschrift der Menschheit,* 9 vols. Leipzig, Germany: Koehler & Amerlang.

Wren, Christopher Jr. 1750. *Parentalia, or, Memoirs of the Family of the Wrens.* London.

Wright, A. R., and T. E. Lones. 1936. *Movable Festivals.* Vol. 1 of *British Calendar Customs.* London: William Glaisher Ltd.

———. 1938. *Fixed Festivals, January–May, Inclusive.* Vol. 2 of *British Calendar Customs.* London: William Glaisher Ltd.

———. 1940. *Fixed Festivals, June–December, Inclusive.* Vol. 3 of *British Calendar Customs.* London: William Glaisher Ltd.

Yeats, William Butler. 1925. *A Vision: An Explanation of Life Founded upon the Writings of Giraldus and upon Certain Doctrines Attributed to Kustaben Luka*. London: T. Werner Laurie.

Yeowell, John. 1982. *Hidden Gods: The Period of Dual Faith in England, 680–1980*. London: Raven Banner Editions.

Young, Anne. 1992. *Paint Roses and Castles: Traditional Narrow Boat Painting for Homes and Boats*. Newton Abbot, England: David and Charles.

Youngs, Susan, ed. 1989. *The Work of Angels: Masterpieces of Celtic Metalwork, 6th–9th Centuries AD*. London: British Museum Publications.

———. 1991. "The Steeple Bumpstead Boss." In *The Age of Migrating Ideas: Early Medieval Art in Northern Britain and Ireland*, ed. R. Michael Spearman and John Higgitt, 143–50. Edinburgh, National Museums of Scotland; Stroud, England: Alan Sutton Publishing.

Ziegler, Gerd. 1986. *Tarot: Mirror of the Soul*. Wellingborough, England: Aquarian Press.

INDEX

Page numbers in *italic* represent illustrations.